Education in Globalization

By
Paul C. Mocombe

UNIVERSITY PRESS OF AMERICA,® INC.
Lanham • Boulder • New York • Toronto • Plymouth, UK

Contents

Acknowledgments   v

Introduction   vii

1   Post-industrial Pedagogy in America, the Hegemon of
Globalization or the Contemporary World-System   1

2   The Sociolinguistic Nature of Black Academic Failure in
Capitalist Education: A Reevaluation of "Language in the
Inner-City" and its Social Function, "Acting White"   15

3   Where Did Freire Go Wrong? Pedagogy in Globalization:
The Grenadian Example   23

4   Toward Democratic Communism: What is to be Done When
'All are Interpellated and "Embourgeoised" Capitalists   31

References   45

Index   53

Acknowledgments

My analysis and conclusions are the result of the mentoring of three great professors, the late Drs. Stanford M. Lyman and Teresa Brennan, and Dr. Susan Love-Brown; to them I owe my intellectual growth and framework. I would also like to thank Dr. Glynn, Dr. Stover, Dr. Headley, Dr. Araghi, and Dr. Nelson, for their help, insight, and patience provided to me during the writing of this work. Lastly, I would like to thank my grandparents, Saul and Eugenia Mocombe, Corliss Ann Russell, and Tiara S. Harris who taught me why and how to love.

Introduction

The upper class of owners and high-level executives, based in the corporate community of developed countries like the United States, represent today's dominant bourgeois capitalist class whose various distributive powers lead to a situation where their policies (discursive practices, i.e., neoliberal policies) determine the "life chances" of not only local social actors, within the globalizing developed nation, but global ones as well. As William Domhoff (2002) points out in *Who Rules America*, "The routinized ways of acting in the United States follow from the rules and regulations needed by the corporate community to continue to grow and make profits" (Domhoff, 2002: 181).

Globally, this action plays out through US dominated institutions such as the World Bank (WB), World Trade Organization (WTO), International Monetary Fund (IMF) etc., who prescribe fiscal, political, and social policies to countries in search of aid for development. These policies aid the corporate-driven agenda of the developed world (fits them within the structure of their social relations, i.e., the discourse of the Protestant ethic and its discursive practice, the Spirit of Capitalism), rather than the agenda of the developing countries: the establishment of "free" open markets as the basis for development and social relations in developing countries, whose markets when established are unable to compete with that of competitors in the West. They therefore get usurped by the capitalists of the West who take advantage of the labor force—which is cheapened in order to compete globally with other—cheaper—prospective markets—and other resources of the developing country, who must allow these investors into their country in order to pay back the debts they owe to the aforementioned international institutions lest they are declared ineligible for aid and development loans if they do not open up (liberalize) and secure their markets.

On one side of the political spectrum, this contemporary trend has been labeled globalization (market-driven as opposed to the post World War II development model, which emphasized economic replication, i.e., prescribed stages of economic development for developing countries, along the lines of the developed world—US and Europe) under the auspices of neoliberalism (McMichael, 1996; Portes, 1997), a common sense view that tends to see globalization as both an ideological force (a conceptualization of the world [, i.e., establishment of markets as the basis for social relations]) and a material force (i.e., real transnational movements of capital and commodities). That is to say, from this "natural attitude" or perspective, globalization serves not only as a tool for investors to extract concessions from states, and for investors and states to extract concessions from workers and other citizens (Klak, 1998: 5), but also as a means of socialization to the capitalist social relations of production as the constitutive "practical consciousness" of modern societies. This is an ideological position, which assumes a distinction between the "life-world" of cultural meanings and subjective experiences, and the capitalist non-cultural, but rational, system, which "organically" governs them as a result of politically arrived at agreements (Habermas, 1984 [1981]).

On the other side of the political spectrum, this same position amounts to a (neo) liberal euphemism for Immanuel Wallerstein's (1974) Marxist world-systems theory, which emphasizes the integration of the world into a functional system "based on capitalist commodity production organized by a world market in which both purely economic competitive advantage and political interference by states play an interactive role" (Chase-Dunn, 1977: 455). In other words, "in the modern world-system there is only one mode of production, commodity production for profit on the world market, that articulates different forms of labor exploitation and encompasses a system of differentially powerful [(core)] states and peripheral areas" (Chase-Dunn, 1977: 455) from whom concessions are extracted and social relations are normalized, regardless of race, ethnicity, gender, and sexuality, to meet the ends (profit-motive) of the capitalist system as driven by one powerful core state, the hegemon, in today's global setting the US being that hegemon.

Whereas the dominant focus of world-systems analysis and the common sense view has been on the exploitative (or not) capitalist material relations between and within core and periphery states, i.e., the attempt of capital operating in and out of core states to increase the rate of profit through the production of surplus-value and consumption of goods from workers in their respective states and those in developing or periphery countries. The point of emphasis here is on the ideological aspect or the integration of this relation in terms of capitalist ideological domination. This is an important distinction in terms of understanding the capitalist system's social integration; while the material approach of the liberal position views the system or structure of capitalist relations as distinct from the plethora of cultural meanings and subjective experiences, which operate within its rational and "organic" systemic framework; my position, in keeping with the structural determinism of the world-system school, argues that the contrary is the norm. That is, the capitalist system, and its structural logic and ethic, colonizes the lifeworld, the world of day-to-day practical action, to prevent differentiation of norms and subjective experiences from that of the "Protestant ethic and the spirit of capitalism."

From this position, the view is that in the emerging post-development global setting (globalization), globalizing capitalist core states, like the US (i.e., the hegemon of the contemporary world-system), no longer rely exclusively on political and military force to extract concessions, or market forces (for that matter) to reproduce the system or the structure of capitalist social relations amongst their citizens and those in periphery nations. Instead, as Louis Althusser points out (2001 [1971]), as governing elites in control of the state, as the constitutive element for bourgeois domination, investors pressure other states to use state "ideological apparatuses" such as education to *inter pellate* (name) and *embourgeois* their "workers and other citizens" with the ideological practices (i.e., discursive practices) that justify, and make acceptable, their role (agents of the Protestant ethic) in the investor/worker relationship that structures the global social relation of production. Through "ideological state apparatuses," such as education, social actors in modern societies are named (interpellated) and given ("embourgeoised" with) the "ethics" and "practical-consciousness" needed for both their "ontological security" and the reproduction of the structural practices needed for the mode of production by which capital seeks to generate surplus-value or accumulate capital.

Thus, "ideological state apparatuses," in essence, become the force-less means of socialization to the dominant capitalist order of things. So that in the case of education as an ideological state apparatus in today's emergent post-industrial global economy and culture, for example, the pedagogical practices and curricula are those, which are required to reproduce the consumerist means of accumulating capital, which dominates the contemporary world-system under American Hegemony. This fact further implies that the transformation of society rests not on the subjective initiatives of *all* social actors, but on the "objective forces" (discourse), i.e., ideals, disseminated through education as an ideological apparatus, which US capital and their pawns (upper and middle transnational class of investors) equate with the nature of reality and existence as such. Hence, whereas those in power positions, investors in the global economy, actively partake in the reproduction and transformation of society and the world around them, by (re) configuring the discursive practices (i.e., rules and regulations of the "Spirit of Capitalism") of the ideology (the Protestant discourse) within which their self-interest is best attainable (See figure I-1). The majority of workers and other citizens (non-investors), at best, become pawns of the ideology, as they recursively organize and reproduce, for their ontological security, the discursive practices of power. This is a seemingly non-agential position, for from this perspective social actors lack the theoretical and practical skills to transform their world as they encounter it; they simply reproduce it (attempting to live as investors) given their indoctrination—"embourgeoisement," in state ideological apparatuses such as education—into the pragmatics of bourgeois living, which exploits and oppresses the many for the expense of the few seeking economic gain for its own sake.

Institutional regulators
(Society's educational/ideological apparatuses)

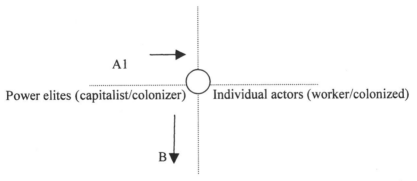

Power elites (capitalist/colonizer)   Individual actors (worker/colonized)

Society's semiotic field

Figure I.1.   Diagram representing the structure of Bourgeois culture. Capitalist interpretations (Marxist, Postmodernist, World-system, and dependency, theories) view the synchronic axis (horizontal line) as resulting from the practices of the diachronic axis (the vertical line). That is, the economic subjugation running along line A1 derives from the abstract laws (neoliberal policies) of institutional regulators (movement of line B), which rigidifies, i.e., reifies, into the horizontal axis and is exported throughout the global (globalization).

My interpretation, in keeping with the structural logic of Max Weber (1958 [1905]), posits that the synchronic axis (Protestantism) gives rise to the diachronic (i.e., historical) practice—vertical axis—, capitalism, and globalization represents the means of localizing or structuring the global setting within the structure, or if you would, discourse of Protestantism, through capitalist practices, whether development (replication) models or market ones.

This work is a collection of new and previous published essays that attempt to understand the sociology of education in the contemporary post-industrial (re) configuration of capitalist power relations under American Hegemony. Chapter 1, "Post-industrial Pedagogy in America, the Hegemon of Globalization or the Contemporary World System," argues that Paulo Freire's dialogical pedagogy, as contemporarily practiced in American post-industrial workplaces and schools, speaks to the continual role of education as an instrument that is used to facilitate integration, rather than as a liberating force against the partiality of its capitalist ideological structure. The essay, through a worldsystems approach, offers a rereading of Freire's emphasis on dialogue, as contemporarily practiced in the American context, which not only refutes it in favor of the antidialogical model or the "Banking system," but demonstrates, contrarily to the poststructural emphasis, how dialogical pedagogy is utilized, within existing configuration of post-industrial capitalist power in the US, to foster normalization (i.e., homogenization) amongst diverse "cultural" identities (race, ethnicity, gender, and sexuality) in the attempt to accumulate surplus-value or economic gain for its own sake.

Chapter 2, "The Sociolinguistic Nature of Black Academic Failure in Capitalist Education: A Reevaluation of 'Language in the Inner-City' and its Social Function, 'Acting White'," through a reexamination of the black-white achievement gap examines the impact of the homogenization process for the accumulation of capital on local minority social actors, in this case on black social actors, who have for centuries borne the burden of the contradiction of capital accumulation. Chapter 3, "Where Did Freire Go Wrong? Pedagogy in Globalization: The Grenadian Example," looks at the homogenization of cultural identity in the contemporary world-system at the global level.

The chapter concentrates specifically on the constitution of Grenadian identity within the investor/worker social relation that constitutes contemporary societies in the American dominated capitalist world-system. Whereas in chapters 1 and 2, I conclude that social actors in the US are educated to work and function within a service-oriented consumerist economy; in chapter 3, I utilize the Grenadian example to demonstrate the role of the citizens of other nation-states in the American dominated world-system. I conclude from this example, that the Grenadians are educated in the American dominated capitalist world-system to work in manufacturing and low-wage tertiary-service industries owned by multi-nationals operating out of the US and Europe, who have transferred these jobs there in the attempt to off-set labor cost.

I conclude the work with the essay, "'Democratic Communism' Against Cosmopolitanism and Identity Politics: What is to be done when all are Interpellated and 'Embourgeoised' Capitalists? This final essay gives an answer, "Democratic Communism," to resolving the most pressing contradiction of capital accumulation, the exploitation of social actors in capitalist social relations in the midst of their commitment to its logic, capital accumulation, as the key to liberation, a paradox which stems from the masses themselves given their embourgeoisement through education as an ideological apparatus for bourgeois domination.

The hope of this work, given the recurring language, ideas, and form which constitutes these individual essays as a book, is to paint a picture of education in contemporary times that highlights its main objective, to name and give all social actors, regardless of race, greed, religion, or ethnicity, the ethics needed to serve the need of capital, capital accumulation, in the midst of one of its pressing contradictory practices, the proletarianization of the masses.

Chapter One

Post-industrial Pedagogy in America, the Hegemon of Globalization or the Contemporary World-System

INTRODUCTION

It is through education, with the rise of the modern state, by which the members of the dominant group, the upper class of owners and high-level executives (bourgeois capitalists) in this day and age, impose their will throughout society (Bowles and Gintis, 1976; Bourdieu, 1973). This suggests, given the "disembeddedness" of the economy from social control as social control, that the educational curriculum (and by association its pedagogical practices) are those which the economic base, as perceived by those in power positions, requires. Thus education, in this sense, becomes the primary means of "enculturation" or "socialization" to participation in life processes in modern times. For by controlling the material resources that sustain institutions, education in this case, the powerful [(capitalists, i.e., upper class of owners and high-level executives)] can deny resources needed to make vital identity claims and to experience selves as agents (Schwalbe, 1993: 342).

"Selves are thus stunted as they are disciplined and harnessed to serve the needs of capital" (Schwalbe, 1993; 342–343). This in essence means, "[t]here is no such thing as a neutral educational process [or essential selves for that matter]. For selves are a product of education that either functions as an instrument that is used to facilitate the integration of the younger generation into the logic of the present system and bring about conformity to it, or it becomes 'the practice of freedom,' the means by which men and women deal critically and creatively with reality and discover how to participate in the transformation of their world" (Freire 2000 [1970]: 34).

But how is this possible? How can education come to serve as "the means by which men and women deal critically and creatively with reality and discover how to participate in the transformation of their world," if, as I am suggesting, it is always an institution of the power structure? The late Brazilian social theorist Paulo Freire (2000 [1970]) suggests that it is through the restructuring of the education system to allow for dialogue between subjective or cultural structural positions prior to the "prescriptive" process where the teacher's dominating knowledge is taught to students.

Recent shifts in American and global pedagogical practices (as a result of the shift from an industrial to a postindustrial economy), which appear to emphasize Freire's dialogical model, however, speaks, as I intend to argue here, to the continual role of education as an instrument that is used to facilitate integration, rather than as a liberating force against what has become a *reified consciousness*, i.e., the global capitalist ideological social structure or culture, which stratifies social actors along class lines and prevents the poor from dealing critically and creatively with reality given their poor status positions in relation to the means of production (Mocombe, 2001).

So where did Freire go wrong? This chapter, and the subsequent chapters to follow, offers a rereading, at the world-system level, of Freire's emphasis on dialogue as contemporarily practiced in the American and (by hegemonic association) global context to normalize divergent discursive practices within the Protestant discourse and its discursive practice, the "Spirit of Capitalism."

THE GLOBAL CONTEXT AND ITS "SOCIAL STRUCTURE OF INEQUALITY"

The upper class of owners and high-level executives, based in the corporate community of developed countries like the United States, represent today's dominant bourgeois capitalist class whose various distributive powers lead to a situation where their policies (economic neo-liberal policies) determine the "life chances" of not only local social actors, within the globalizing developed nation, but global ones as well. As William Domhoff (2002) points out in *Who Rules America*, "The routinized ways of acting in the United States follow from the rules and regulations needed by the corporate community to continue to grow and make profits" (Domhoff, 2002: 181). Globally, this action plays out through US dominated institutions such as the World Bank (WB), World Trade Organization (WTO), International Monetary Fund (IMF) etc., who prescribe fiscal, political, and social policies to countries in search of aid for development that aids the corporate-driven agenda of the developed world (that is, fits them within the structure of their social relations, i.e., the discourse of the Protestant ethic and its discursive practice, the Spirit of Capitalism), rather than the agenda of the developing countries: the establishment of open markets as the basis for development and social relations in developing countries, whose markets when established are unable to compete with that of competitors in the West, and therefore get usurped by the capitalists of the West who take advantage of the labor force—which is cheapened and exploited in order to compete globally with other—cheaper—prospective markets—and other resources of the developing country, who must allow these investors into their country in order to pay back the debts they owe to the aforementioned international institutions, lest they be declared ineligible for aid and development loans if they do not open up (liberalize) and secure their markets.

On one side of the political spectrum, this contemporary trend has been labeled globalization under the auspices of neoliberalism, a common sense view that tends to see globalization as both an ideological force (a conceptualization of the world [i.e., establishment of markets as the basis for social relations]) and a material force (i.e., real transnational movements of capital and commodities) (McMichael, 1996; Portes, 1997; Klak, 1998). That is to say, from this "natural attitude" or perspective globalization serves not only as a tool for investors to extract concessions from states, and for investors and states to extract concessions from workers and other citizens, but also as a means of socialization to the capitalist social relations of production as the constitutive "practical consciousness" of modern societies—an ideological position, which assumes a distinction between the "life-world" of cultural meanings and subjective experiences; and the capitalist non-cultural system, which as a result of mutually arrived at political agreements "organically" governs them (Habermas, 1987 [1981], 1984 [1981]).

On the other side of the political spectrum, this same position amounts to a liberal euphemism for Immanuel Wallerstein's world-systems theory, which emphasizes the integration of the world into a functional system "based on capitalist commodity production organized by a world market in which both purely economic competitive advantage and political interference by states play an interactive role" (Chase-Dunn, 1977: 455). In other words, "in the modern world-system there is only one mode of production, commodity production for profit on the world market, that articulates different forms of labor exploitation and encompasses a system of differentially powerful [(core)] states and peripheral areas" (Chase-Dunn, 1977: 455) from whom concessions are extracted and social relations are normalized, regardless of race, ethnicity, gender, and sexuality, to meet the ends (profit-motive) of the capitalist system as driven by one powerful core state, the hegemon. In today's global setting the US is that hegemon.

Whereas the dominant focus of world-systems analysis and the common sense view has been on the exploitative (or not) material (market) relations between, and within, core and periphery states, the point of emphasis here is on the ideological aspect or the integration of this relation in terms of capitalist ideological domination. This is an important distinction in terms of understanding the nature of social and system integration, for while the material approach of the liberal position views the system or structure of capitalist relations as distinct from the plethora of cultural meanings and subjective experiences, which "organically" operate within its global politico-economic systemic framework (Habermas, 1987 [1981], 1984 [1981]). My position, in keeping with the structural determinism of the world-system position, posits that the contrary is the norm. That is, the capitalist system, and its structural logic, "mechanically" colonizes the lifeworld, the world of day-to-day practical action, to prevent differentiation of norms and subjective experiences from that of "the Protestant ethic and the spirit of capitalism."

From this position, the view is that in the emerging post-development global setting (globalization), globalizing capitalist core states, like the US (i.e., the hegemon of the contemporary world-system), no longer rely exclusively on political and military force to extract concessions, or "market" forces for that matter to reproduce the system or the structure of capitalist social relations amongst their citizens and those in periphery nations.

Instead, as Louis Althusser points out (2001 [1971]), as governing elites in control of the state, as the constitutive element for bourgeois domination, investors pressure other states to use state "ideological apparatuses" such as education to *interpellate* (name) and embourgeois their "workers and other citizens" with the ideological practices that justify, and make acceptable, their role (agents of the Protestant ethic of the calling) in the investor/worker relationship that structures the global social relation of production. In other words, through "ideological state apparatuses," such as education, social actors in modern societies are named (interpellated) and given (embourgeoised with) the "ethics" needed for both their "ontological security" and the reproduction of the structural terms (i.e., norms, values, prescriptions and proscriptions) of the capitalist social relations of production.

Thus, "ideological state apparatuses," in essence, become the force-less means of enculturation or socialization to the dominant capitalist labor order of things. So that in the case of education as an ideological state apparatus in today's emergent global economy and culture, for example, the pedagogical practices and curricula are those, which are required to reproduce the capitalist social relation of production as practiced by the structural agents (the governing bourgeois class of owners and high-level executives in developed countries) of its discourse. This fact further implies that the transformation of society rests not on the subjective initiatives of *all* social actors, but on the "objective forces" (discourse), i.e., ideals, disseminated through education as an ideological apparatus, which these elites equate with the nature of reality and existence as such.

Hence, whereas those in power positions, investors in the global economy, actively partake in the reproduction and transformation of society and the world around them, by (re) configuring the discursive practices (i.e., rules and regulations of the "Spirit of Capitalism") of the ideology (the Protestant discourse) within which their self-interest is best attainable (See figure 1.1).

Institutional regulators
(Society's educational/ideological apparatuses)

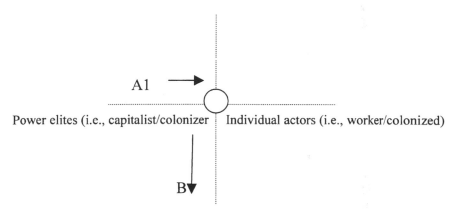

Society's semiotic field

Figure 1.1. Diagram representing the structure of Bourgeois culture. Capitalist interpretations (Marxist, Postmodernist, World-system, and dependency, theories) view the synchronic axis (horizontal line) as resulting from the practices of the diachronic axis (the vertical line). That is, the economic subjugation running along line A1 derives from the abstract laws (neoliberal policies) of institutional regulators (movement of line B), which rigidifies, i.e., reifies, into the horizontal axis and is exported throughout the global (globalization).
My interpretation, in keeping with the structural logic of Ferdinand De Saussure (1986 [1916]: 80) and the "iron cage" thesis of Max Weber (1958 [1905]) posits that the synchronic axis (Protestantism) gives rise to the diachronic (i.e., historical) practice—vertical axis—, capitalism, and globalization represent the means of localizing or structuring the global setting within the structure, or if you would, discourse of Protestantism, through capitalist practices, whether development (replication) models or market ones. So in essence, the Protestant ethic of the calling is the reason for the form of capitalist practices that dominate modernity contemporarily.

The majority of workers and other citizens (non-investors), at best, become pawns of the ideology, as they recursively organize and reproduce, for their *ontological security*, the discursive practices of power. A seemingly non-agential position, for from this perspective social actors lack the theoretical and practical skills to *transform* their world as they encounter it, they simply *reproduce* it (attempting to live as investors), given their indoctrination— "embourgeoisement," in state ideological apparatuses such as education— into the pragmatics of bourgeois living, in spite of the class stratification it (the capitalist social structure) produces.

The emerging post-development or post-industrial global capitalist economy and culture (consumerism), dominated by U.S. foreign policy agenda, and the subsequent transformation of educational pedagogical practices throughout the globe (Tye, 1999)[1], I argue here through an understanding of the dynamics of American pedagogical practices in education as an "ideological state apparatus," speak to this phenomenon of cultural or structural homogenization. This view diametrically opposes the position of most contemporary critical theorists of education, who argue for and attempt to demonstrate cultural heterogeneity (i.e., cultural heterogeneous groups engaged, through pedagogical practices that allow for dialogue) in struggles over the production, legitimation, and circulation of particular forms of meaning and experience, within education as a reproductive apparatus for economic conditions (Erevelles, 2000).

(POST) MODERN PEDAGOGY

In essence, my argument is that it is only under the auspices of contemporary economic conditions (post-industrial consumerist globality) under US hegemony that "contemporary" critical theorists of education are able to speak of cultural heterogeneity within the existing configuration of capitalist labor power relations. In other words, globalism, globalization/world-system, is a condition of present-day US capitalist organization. The process is simply the continual "expansion" of capitalist discursive practices (mostly American dominated), which as Immanuel Wallerstein (1974) points out has always been global in character, across time and space.

As many globalization theorists of the postmodernist variety have demonstrated (Bell, 1976; Harvey, 1989; Giddens, 1990; Jameson, 1991; Arrighi, 1994; Sklair, 2001; Kellner, 2001), however, this contemporary (1970 to the present) condition is no longer characterized or driven by the industrial means for accumulating capital, which dominated the social relations of production of the last one hundred years, instead, the present globalization condition is driven-by, post-industrialism (consumerism)—the new means for accumulating capital—, and in such "developed" societies like the U.S., is characterized not by the industrial organization of labor, but rather by capitalist service occupations catering to the consumerist demands of a dwindling (transnational) middle class.

The rate of economic gain for its own sake or profit has fallen in industrial production due to labor laws and ecological cost in developed countries like the US; hence the practice now among investors operating out of the US is on financial expansion "in which 'over-accumulated' capital switches from investments in production and trade, to investments in finance, property titles, and other claims on future income" (Trichur, 2005: 165).

Globally, the economic bifurcation defining this current conjuncture is characterized, on the one hand, by an expansion of industrial production into developing or periphery and semi-periphery countries (China, Brazil, Mexico, India, and South Africa), where the rate of labor exploitation has risen given their lack of labor laws; and, on the other, consumerism of cheaply produced goods and high-end service occupations has come to dominate developed societies (US, Western Europe, Japan, and Australia).

Socially, the major emphasis among governing elites in this US dominated global economy or social relation of production has been participation or integration of "others" (specifically "hybrids") into the existing configuration of power relations in order to accumulate profits by servicing the diverse financial wants and needs of commodified cultural groups, throughout the globe. A select few live a "bourgeois" middle and upper middle class lifestyle at the expense of the masses working in low-wage agricultural, manufacturing, and production jobs or not at all given the transfer of these jobs overseas to developing countries.

Given that most critical theorists of education have denounced the liberal claim, which sees education as a neutral process, the contemporary debates in educational theory, regarding the role of education in this post-industrial age, which emphasizes global participation (of a transnational middle class), have centered on the degree to which education serves as a reproductive apparatus for economic conditions as opposed to a democratically constructed "discursive space that involves asymmetrical relations of power where both dominant and subordinate groups are engaged in struggles over the production, legitimation, and circulation of particular forms of meaning and experience" (Erevelles, 2000: 30). Peter McLaren (1988) and Henry Giroux (1992), most conspicuously, given the push for educational reform in consumerist globality, which emphasize participatory pedagogical practices such as cooperative group work and other supposedly cultural specific modes of learning, "have begun to examine the discursive practices by which student subjectivity (as constructed by race, class, gender, and sexuality) is produced, regulated, and even resisted within the social context of schooling in postindustrial times" (Erevelles, 2000: 25).

Thus, challenging the claims of Samuel Bowles and Herbert Gintis (1976), for example, who in *Schooling in Capitalist America* argued "that the history of public education in capitalist America was a reflection of the history of the successes, failures, and contradictions of capitalism itself. In other words, they conceptualized schools as "ideological state apparatuses," that, rather than attempting to meet the needs of citizens, instead devised administrative, curricular, and pedagogical practices that reproduced subject positions that sustained [the] exploitative class hierarch[y of capitalism]" (Erevelles, 2000: 28).

McLaren and Giroux, on the contrary, argue that Bowles and Gintis, along with other reproduction theorists such as Basil Bernstein, Pierre Bourdieu, and Immanuel Wallerstein are too deterministic. Hence, influenced by the impact of poststructural theory on cultural studies, McLaren and Giroux among others, instead explore how the everyday actions and cultural practices of students that constitute several subcultures within schools, serve as cultural sites that exist in opposition to the hegemonic dictates of capitalist education (Erevelles, 2000: 30).

My argument in keeping with the structural logic of Gintis, Bowles, Bourdieu, and Wallerstein is that the Freirean dialogical practices, which McLaren and Giroux emphasize as evidential of the democratic struggle, between diverse groups, over the "production, legitimation, and circulation of particular forms of meaning and experience" within the existing hegemony of post-industrial capitalist education, are in fact the result of the social relations of production in post-industrial capital, and therefore paradoxically serves capitalist education.

The consumerist globality of postindustrial capital fosters the participation of the cultural sites that exist in opposition to the dictates of capitalist education. These sites, that is the meaning and new identities allowed to be constructed within the capitalist social space, are used to extract surplus value from their consumer representatives. In other words, cultural sites under US economic global hegemony become markets, structured (through education) within the dictates of the protestant ethic and the spirit of capitalism, to be served, by their predestined (capitalist class) "hybrid" representatives, who, working for the upper-class of owners and high-level executives, service their respective "other" community as petit-bourgeois middle class "hybrid" agents of the Protestant ethic who generate surplus-value, for global capital, through the consumption of cheaply produced products coming out of periphery or developing nations. No longer is the "other" alienated and marginalized by capital; instead they (i.e., those who exercise their "otherness" as hybrids) are embraced and commodified so that the more socialized of their agents can (i.e., through hard work, calculating rationality, etc.) obtain economic gain for its own sake while oppressing the underclass of their communities. These hybrids, characterized by their ethnic middle class-ness, are pawns for capital; they increase the rate of profit for capital through consumption, and by servicing the desires, wants, and needs of the oppressed of their communities as workers (pawns) for the upper class of owners and high-level executives. This is why current pedagogical practices, which reflect Paulo Freire's emphasis on dialogue, lack the potential, contrarily to Freire's inference, for liberation as they are utilized to reproduce the social relations of production under post-industrial global capitalism amongst previously discriminated against "others," the majority of whom remain oppressed given their lack of social and economic capital due to the "expansion" of industrial production (i.e., loss of jobs to developing countries) and the rise of labor exploitation in developing countries.[2]

(POST) INDUSTRIAL PEDAGOGY IN THE US

So the argument here is that critical theorists of education such as McLaren and Giroux under analyze the role of subcultures within education as an ideological apparatus for post-industrial US dominated capital. In other words, they fail to explain the role of subcultures within education as a continuous ideological space for capital. Had they done so, it would be clear that the social relations of production of the two most recent conditions of capitalism are diametrical opposites to say the least, and therefore treat subcultures differently.

Under industrial capitalism, for example, "the scientific management movement initiated by Frederick Winslow Taylor in the last decades of the nineteenth century was brought into being . . . in an attempt to apply the methods of science to the increasingly complex problems of the control of labor [(in order to maximize profits)] in rapidly growing capitalist enterprises" (Braverman, 1998: 59). The end result of this movement was the separation of the roles of worker and management. In the case of post-industrialism (globalization), there was a renewed emphasis on cooperation between worker and management. In both cases, interestingly enough, the techniques and functions of the work place were replicated in US classrooms to serve as the means of socialization or enculturation to the labor process, and its subsequent way of life.

This direct correlation, most conspicuously, was between the implementation of pedagogical practices in American classrooms that paralleled the organization of work under each mode of production (Mocombe, 2001). For instance, under the scientific movement of the industrial stage, mental work was separated from manual work, and "a necessary consequence of this separation [was] that the labor process [became] divided between separate sites and separate bodies of workers. In one location, the physical processes of production [were] executed. In another [were] concentrated the design, planning, calculation, and record-keeping. The preconception of the process before it is set in motion, the visualization of each worker's activities before they have actually begun, the definition of each function along with the manner of its performance and the time it will consume, the control and checking of the ongoing process once it is under way, and the assessment of results upon completion of each stage of the process—all of these aspects of production [were] removed from the shop floor to the management office" (Braverman, 1998;86).

To parallel the concepts of control adopted by management at that time, school curricula in the US stressed marching, drill, orderliness, assigned seats in rows, individualized seatwork, and tracking and leveling; seemingly all were preparation for the coordination and orderliness required in the modern factory. Lining up for class as well as marching in and out of the cloakroom and to the blackboard were activities justified in terms of training for factory assembly lines, while tracking and leveling sorted out future workers and managers (Springs, 1994: 18).

In short, all of the above-mentioned vestiges of the school curriculum/ pedagogy complimented an aspect of the factory under scientific-management. This is why, the service-oriented (post-industrialism) re-structuring of American capitalist society, beginning in the 1960s, witnessed massive reform initiatives in school pedagogies—a result of the re-conceptualization of the role of the worker in the labor-process under consumerist globality. Skills that were peculiar to the industrial worker become futile to the service worker in the postindustrial process. That is, whereas, the old work process was founded on passive submission to schedules or routines, individualism, isolationism, and privatism; the postindustrial or globalization stage of the labor process focuses on teamwork. "It celebrates sensitivity to others; it requires such 'soft skills' as being a good listener and being cooperative" (Sennett, 1998: 99).

This reorganization of work has revamped the role of the laborer in the work process, and "throughout the U.S. economy, employers and managers are promoting a new ethos of participation for their workers. In fact, the spread of a paradigm of participation—comprised of extensive discussion about the merits of worker involvement as well as actual transformation of production methods and staffing practices—may indeed be one of the most significant trends sweeping across postindustrial, late twentieth-century workplaces" (Smith, 1998: 460).

To ensure socialization to this new aspect of *Being* in capitalism, this trend of employee involvement is adumbrated in the pedagogical curriculum reform movements of many US school systems, which place a major emphasis on "process approaches," "active learning strategies," such as cooperative learning, group work, and many other "soft skills"—good listener, speaker, and writer—which characterize the dialogical elements of the new labor-process.[3]

This paradigm of participation, accordingly, is not an attempt on behalf of management to reassociate the conception of work with its execution. In other words, this is neither a reconstruction of Taylorism's principles nor a means of trying to liberate the workers, as a result of the subsequent dialogue brought on by this ethos of participation. Instead, "Sociologists, industrial relations researchers, organizational scientists, and policymakers who have studied this trend agree that leaders and managers of U.S. companies are climbing aboard the bandwagon of worker participation in their urgent attempts to maintain competitiveness under changing economic circumstances. Employers believe that when workers participate in making decisions, when they gain opportunities to apply their tacit knowledge to problem solving, and when they acquire responsibility for designing and directing production processes, they feed into an infrastructure enabling firms to respond to shifting market and product demands [(consumer demands)] in a rapid and timely way" (Smith, 1998: 460).

This is the fundamental reason why the existing configurations of economic hegemonic power, located in the US contemporarily, allow for the fashioning and participation of new identities (through pedagogical practices that engender participation, i.e., cooperative group work, field trips, class room presentations, etc.) in the order of things: under industrial capitalism the aim of the upper-class of owners and high level executives was accumulation of capital through the industrial production of cheaply produced goods for the dominating masses and those in militarily controlled overseas markets (hence the rise of surplus-value at the expense of labor exploitation in industrial jobs); under post-industrialism, however, the emphasis is servicing a larger segment of these markets, not just the initial colonial "hybrid" petit-bourgeois class, who are also interested in obtaining a larger portion of these markets as members of a dwindling (transnational) middle class interpellated by, and "embourgeoised" with the wants and needs of, capital (hence the fall of the rate of profit). This middle class, which is a result of the restructuring of the organization of labor (service-oriented in the First World or core nations, production in the Third or developing world) by the dominant bourgeois class of owners and high-level executives in core countries in order to increase the rate of profit or accumulate more capital, constitute the capitalist social space as pawns or service-workers, who service the desires, wants, and needs of the oppressed of their respective communities—who are either unemployed or work in labor intensive production jobs—while at the same time legitimating the "hybrid" petit-bourgeois middle class identity, which the oppressed, working in low-wage earning occupations or not at all, must aspire to, and producing surplus value (increasing the rate of profit) for capital through consumption.

Thus, in the socialization of "identities-in-differential" within education as an ideological apparatus for the post-industrial capitalist social structure what is (re) produced is ideological sameness amongst diverse "bodies/subjects" vying for control of their commodified oppressed markets as firms, who employ the more integrated or socialized amongst them, "hybrids," learn, by using the knowledge which dialogue between subjective positions foster, how to maximize their profits by catering to the needs of these "new" consumers represented by "hybrids," i.e., "other" agents of the protestant ethic and the spirit of capitalism, of their communities.

Thus, the introduction of management-initiated employee involvement programs (EIPs), as well as paralleling pedagogical practices (dialogue, multiculturalism, "soft skills," i.e., good listener, etc.) in schools, have been introduced, under the auspices and practical consciousness of the "hybrid" class of once discriminated against identities, who have sided with capital, in order to obtain profit through auxiliary service occupations—consumerism, the current means of capital accumulation, currently dominating the globalization process or, as Wallerstein three decades ago framed it, the "world-economy"—controlled by capital, who continues to oppress and marginalize the poor it creates in developing countries through the outsourcing of low-wage production jobs to keep down the cost of labor and extract surplus-value.

In this sense, education is no longer a discursive space where student subjectivity, as constructed by race, class, gender, and sexuality is given free reign to develop; on the contrary, their subjectivity, as constructed by race, class, gender, and sexuality is (re) produced and regulated by hybrid bourgeois constructions determined by their relation to the means of production. The case of the black American at the micro-social level illustrates this aforementioned point.

NOTES

1. Kenneth A. Tye (1999), the foremost authority on global education curriculum, in his analysis of global education, *Global Education: A Worldwide Movement*, in the globalization process, points to two ways in which the globalization movement is re-

lated to or correlates with education: curriculum content and pedagogical techniques. In an analysis in which he surveys the curriculum content and pedagogical techniques of schools in 52 countries, Tye highlights elements of the content and teaching techniques emphasized by the schools that reflect or stresses the modernist drive toward "regional and international cooperation and the integration of ecological, economic, political, technological, and even cultural systems of the world" (1). According to Tye, global education curriculum content stress the infusion of global perspectives, ideas and activities into existing curricula (among these the environment, development, intercultural relations, peace, economics, technology, and human rights are the issues most often identified), while the pedagogical techniques focus on how to disseminate that information, i.e., traditionally or using newer, more progressive Methodologies.

Traditional methods of instruction range from "very traditional (teacher lectures, assigns text readings, gives students practice exercises or questions to answers, test students) to more modern (i.e., use of film, video, photographs, transparencies, other audio-visuals)" (68–69). On the other hand, more progressive methodologies (which reflects Freire's dialogical pedagogy), according to Tye, employ "process approaches", "active learning strategies", "inquiry", and "discovery" (i.e., role play and simulations, cooperative learning and group work, thematic curriculum planning, project method, travel programs, and use of technology). Tye attributes the relationship between the content of school curriculums and pedagogical techniques to that of function; pedagogical methods serve the function of distributing curriculum content information. Although Tye suggests that "global education advocates pretty much prescribe a wide range of the progressive methods for use by classroom teachers" (94), his analysis fails to point out the reason(s) why a shift in pedagogical methodology is required in globalization; for it appears that the traditional methods are just as capable of distributing the content information of global education as the progressive methods.

2. My reading of globalization completely breaks away from critical social theorists (Gilder 1989, 2000; Kaku, 1997; Kellner), who see globalization as an integral part of the scientific and technological revolutions of the modern era. I believe it is not necessarily the case that the scientific and technological revolutions of the modern era should give rise to present global processes; in fact, the networking of people, ideas, forms of culture, and people across national boundaries has been an integral aspect of human culture. So much so, that I would venture to call it a natural process. Thus, for me, "modern" globalization is a movement whereby a dominant culture, i.e., bourgeois capitalist culture of the West (America and Western Europe), attempts to reproduce its way of life by integrating the world's population into its structures of signification, i.e., freedom, democracy, increased wealth, and happiness (the protestant ethic). All of this is accomplished through a set of social relations directed and controlled by the market, military power, and supervisory institutions such as the U.N.

3. Essentially, this is also the basis for contemporary struggles over educational testing reform, i.e., the necessary push to reassess and reconfigure the testing tools within post-industrial societies.

Chapter Two

The Sociolinguistic Nature of Black Academic Failure in Capitalist Education: A Reevaluation of "Language in the Inner-City" and its Social Function, "Acting White"

AMERICAN BLACKS IN THE CAPITALIST SOCIAL STRUCTURE

American Blacks, as interpellated (workers) and embourgeoised agents of the American capitalist social structure, represent the most modern (i.e. socialized) people of color, in terms of their "practical consciousness," in this process of homogenizing social actors as agents of the protestant ethic or disciplined workers working for owners of production in order to obtain economic gain for its own sake (Frazier, 1957; Wilson, 1978; Glazer and Moynihan, 1963). They constitute the social space in terms of their relation to the means of production in post-industrial capitalist America, which differentiates black America into two status groups, a dwindling middle class (living in suburbia) that numbers about 25 percent of their population and obtain their status as doctors, lawyers, teachers, entertainers, athletes, and other high-end service occupations; and a growing segregated "black underclass" of unemployed and under-employed wage-earners occupying poor inner-city communities and schools focused solely on multicultural entertaining (i.e., diversity), athletics, and test-taking for social promotion.

Consequently, the poor performance of their children in education as an ideological apparatus for this capitalist sociolinguistic worldview leaves them disproportionately in this growing underclass at the bottom of the social structure unable to either transform their world as they encounter it, or truly exercise their embourgeoisement given their lack of, what sociologist Pierre Bourdieu (1973, 1984) refers to as, capital (cultural, social, economic, and political).[1]

Paradoxically, it is due to their indigent (pathological-pathogenic) structural position within the capitalist social structure, as opposed to a differing cultural ethos from that of the latter, as to the reason why they fail. In other

words, I am not positing that the black child, as a result of the poverty brought
on by the relational logic or differentiation of capitalist social relations, de-
velops cultural norms, which diametrically oppose the "protestant ethic and
the spirit of capitalism" of the society; to the contrary, the black child's culture of poverty is a result of their embodiment of bourgeois ideals amidst poor
or meager material conditions in urban inner-cities. Thus, the logic here is
that the majority of black children fail in school in general and on standardized tests in particular, not because they possess or are taught (by their peers)
at an early age distinct normative values from that of the dominant social
structure that transfer into cultural and political conflict in the classroom, as
an ideological apparatus for capitalists.

On the contrary, black children fail in school because in acquiring the "verbal behavior" of the dominant social structure in segregated "poor" inner-city
communities and schools which lack resources, the majority, who happen to
be less educated in the "Standard English" of the society, have reinforced a
linguistic community or status group as the bearers of ideological and linguistic domination for black America. Thus, it is due to "a mismatch of linguistic structures" and the functional conflicts of standard and nonstandard
English as to the reason many black students disproportionally do poorly on
standardized tests in particular and in school in general.

BLACKS IN CAPITALIST EDUCATION

Traditional theories, building on the cultural-ecological approach of John
Ogbu, have argued that blacks given their racial marginalization within the
socioeconomic/racial social structure either developed an oppositional social
"identity-in-differential" that defined "certain activities, events, symbols, and
meanings as not appropriate for them because those behaviors, events, symbols, and meanings are characteristic of white Americans" (Fordham and
Ogbu 1986: 181), or they stem from a culture of poverty that devalues educational attainment (Sowell, 1975, 1981; Murray, 1984).

My argument posits that "the burden of acting white"—which claims that
"the choice between representing an authentic 'black' self and striving for academic success creates a 'burden of acting white' and contributes to the rela-
tively low academic performance of black students" (Tyson et al, 2005:
584)—and the culture of poverty positions are false characterizations of the
social phenomenon affecting black academic failure. Instead, the reason is
more cognitive than social, and the sociocultural phenomenon of "acting
white" is because of the functional conflicts between sociolinguistic commu-

nities as opposed to a "black" culture of poverty that devalues education (for a somewhat similar argument, see Tyson et al, 2005).[2]

In order to adequately understand the phenomenon of black academic failure or underachievement in relation to whites, from this class-based perspective, in other words, it is not enough to emphasize how so-called cultural norms of the status group affected somehow "magically" (the sociological fallacy) effect cognitive processes of the individual social actor. To the contrary, it should be the converse; the emphasis should be on the cognition of the individual social actor, the black child, and secondarily the impact of the social milieu on that cognition. This process is brilliantly highlighted in William Labov's work *Language in the Inner-City: Studies in the Black English Vernacular* (1972).

FRAMING THE PROBLEM

To understand this relationship between class stratification and the dilemma of the lack of high achievement amongst blacks, I focus on the sociolinguistic nature of black academic failure in K–12 education. William Labov (1972), *Language in the Inner-City: Studies in the Black English Vernacular*, was one of the first scholars in the social sciences to tackle this issue from such a viewpoint. Labov argues that although the cultural or normative differences between blacks and whites are real, from the systematicity of Black English to the functional behavior it engenders, these differences are not the reason black inner city youth fail in school or score poorly on standardized tests. According to Labov, the reason for black underachievement is more systemic or organizational; that is, black students fail because of the class and racial marginalization (i.e., "poor schools," "tracking," "ability teaching," and "poor curricular materials") they experience in the classroom.

Such tendencies lead to poor performances in school in general, and on standardized tests in particular, because it follows that the class and racial biases of teachers and administrators structure "black" schools as though they are attended by more "difficult" and "lower ability" students who take up much of the teaching time; so, they divert school resources toward classroom management (entertaining them to keep them passive) and athletics, rather than curricula that cover content (Van Hook, 2002; Dreeben and Barr, 1983; Bankston and Caldas, 1996; Labov, 1972).

For Labov, the cultural or racial differences, in order to prevent the academic bias currently dominating schools, should be incorporated in the classroom through culturally sensitive curricula to ameliorate the sociocultural strife internalized by black students, which leads to their oppositional world-view, the "burden of acting white," to the ethos of schooling, and subsequent failure on standardized tests in particular and school in general. In sum, Labov argues that the linguistic (BEV) and cultural differences in black inner-city communities should not be marginalized by teachers and administrators, but must be utilized to facilitate the teachings of the dominant culture. This, he concludes, will narrow the black-white "racial divide" in student achievement.

It is my position, however, given the continuing poor performance of black inner city youth in school (for entertainment and athletics) in general, and on reading standardized tests in particular, in spite of recent pushes throughout the nation for culturally sensitive curricula given the society's shift to post-industrialism, that the issue is less cultural or cultural conflict in the classic anthropological or sociological sense as highlighted by Labov, and more sociolinguistic, i.e., "mismatch of linguistic structures and functions" (Labov, 1972: 6) in a—class-based—structurally differentiated sense.

In other words, Labov gets it wrong in trying to draw a correlation between "racialized" structural differentiation, produced by a once racialized American capitalist social structure, and academic failure amongst black youth. The "locus of causality," given the ever "declining significance of race," (Wilson, 1978) is more cognitive, and the disparities in achievement where they exists rest on the class differentiation produced by the American post-industrial capitalist social structure rather than racial marginalization (U.S. Department of Education, 2003).[3]

More black children fail in school, more so than their white or Asian counterparts, not because the majority of blacks are inherently inferior or purposely fail because they feel alienated by the racist practices in the classroom. On the contrary, they perform poorly because they are socialized in a sociolinguistic status group (i.e., the black underclass, which is a result of poverty brought on by the class structural differentiation of American capitalism), which fosters a "deep linguistic structure," (i.e., Black English Vernacular—BEV) that, as Labov brilliantly highlights, is systemically different from the linguistic one (Standard English) which the dominant group in the society seeks to foster through education as an "ideological state apparatus." As a result, the majority of black students, who possess "inherent ability" and identify with the black sociolinguistic group, fail due to either: 1) a "mismatch of linguistic structures" (k–5th grade)[4], or 2) "mismatch in the functions of BEV and Standard English (5th and up).

In other words, black children do poorly on standardized tests in particular and school in general early on in their academic careers, because the poor status group, "black underclass," created by the social relations of capitalism, establishes a sociolinguistic status group that reinforces a linguistic structure (Black English Vernacular—BEV), which renders its young social actors impotent in classrooms where the structure of standard English is taught. Hence early on (k–5th), many black inner city youth struggle in the classroom and on standardized tests because they are having a problem with comprehension, i.e., "a mismatch in linguistic structure."

Later on in their academic careers as these youth become adolescents, they are further disadvantaged by the social functions (a mismatch of function of the language) this status group reinforces. That is, success or economic gain amongst this "black underclass," who speak BEV, is not measured by status obtained through education (that is not the essence of their educational experiences) as in the case of black and white bourgeois middle class standards; on the contrary, athletics, music, and other activities not "associated" with "traditional" educational attainment serve as the means to success. Thus, effort in school (for academic achievement) in general suffers, and as a result test scores and grades are low. This is what many bourgeois scholars (Ogbu, 1974, 1990, 1991; Coleman, 1988) incorrectly interpret as "the burden of act ing white" amongst black adolescents, who as they get older turn away from "traditional" academic education, not because they feel it is for "White folks," but due to the fact that they have rationalized other racializing (i.e., sports, music, pimping, selling drugs, etc.) means to economic gain for its own sake other than bourgeois status obtained through academics.

Hence where I disagree with Labov's work is in its macro conclusions. William Labov's claim in *Language in the Inner-City: Studies in the Black English Vernacular* (1972) that it is unlikely that the structures of BEV "could be responsible for the disastrous record of reading failure in the inner city schools" (Labov, 1972: 241) grossly overestimates, as do the aforementioned (Fordham and Ogbu, 1986; Bergin and Cooks, 2002; Ford and Harris, 1996; Sowell, 1975, 1981; Murray, 1984) qualitative studies, cultural and political conflict as the major cause of that failure.

Labov, in attempting to correlate what amounts to racial conflict in the classroom with poor academic performance amongst blacks in the inner-city, dismisses the obvious causal impact that the cognition associated with the distinct linguistic systemacity of Black English Vernacular, which he argues teachers should take into account when teaching, would and should have on the performance of an irreducibly situated black child independently taking a test to measure his/her academic performance or achievement.

For Labov, the black child, having a distinct cultural background from that of their predominantly white teachers or for that matter black middle class teachers, somehow internalize this cultural conflict (racial if one reads into the work) when taking an independently given test to the point that their nihilistic attitude about the American social structure curbs their effort in taking these tests which results in their poor (or underachieved) performances.

I find it absurd to believe that the systemacity of Black English Vernacular, i.e., deletion and contraction of the copula, non-usage of the historical present, "no present copula or auxiliary *be*," which Labov recognizes is in many regards structurally distinct from the Standard English of the upper class of owners and high-level executives who determine the life chances of all social actors in this day and age, is somehow not directly correlated with success on "reading" standardized tests in particular and school in general. In other words, Labov has not demonstrated conclusively how a black student, who is socialized in a "distinct" linguistic community (the black underclass) that reinforces, for example, statements like, "He done kick me"; "he kick," for historical past and present; "he be like that, kickin me" satisfactorily comprehends (i.e., linguistically matches) "he kicked me;" "he kicks" vs. "he kicked," for historical past and present; "he likes to kick me" when strung together to form essays and questions on standardized tests.

This "mismatch in linguistic structure" is the driving force behind the black/white achievement gap. To name one more example corroborating this point, in the high stakes Florida Comprehensive Assessment test (FCAT), 2004–2005 school year, 64 percent of white students, grades 3 through 10, scored at or above grade level in reading, while 35 percent of African American students scored at or above grade level (Florida Department of Education, 2005). The disparities on the reading test were greatest not in overall reading content area, but in words/phrases recognition and recognizing main idea/author's purpose where whites tended to do significantly better than blacks. On average the majority white schools tended to score 5 out of 7 on words/phrases recognition and 15 out of 24 on main idea/author's purpose; black schools, conversely, averaged 4 or below and 13 or below, respectively (Florida Department of Education, 2005).

CONCLUSIONS

Although the obvious disparity in elements of reading that emphasize comprehension further highlights this "mismatch of linguistic structure" alluded to above, it is not, however, the same thing as saying that BEV does not, given its systemacity, allow a black child to critically think, or that "[b]lack children from the ghetto area . . . receive little verbal stimulation. . . . hear very little well-formed language, and as a result are impoverished in their means of verbal expression" (Labov, 1972: 201).

To the contrary, my position is that whereas speakers of BEV are able to verbally articulate rational and analytical thinking within their linguistic community, as Labov demonstrates in his participant observations; my argument is that "black children" from the ghetto area receive that great deal of verbal stimulation and participate fully in that highly verbal culture directed by not your black middle class pawns of the capitalist social structure who control and utilize the education system as a means to obtain status, but structurally differentiated pawns, i.e., the black underclass, who serve as a status group, for the larger black community, and promulgate a pathological-pathogenic dialect (which has been recognized in the academy as a standard language given its institutionalization amongst the "black underclass") of Standard English. This BEV (Black English Vernacular) reinforced by the black underclass renders its speakers linguistically impotent in the classroom of their oppressors, i.e., the upper class of owners and high level executives and the black bourgeoisie or middle class, when they initially enter school, while offering status based on its function in music, sports, etc. later on in life under post-industrial capital domination.

In either case black youth are unable to be in the world as rational agents in charge of their own destiny, for in both cases they exist as a "class-in-itself" directed on the one hand by a "class-for-itself" (i.e., black bourgeoisie or middle class) operating through school as an ideological apparatus for their capitalist interest; and on the other hand, they are directed by a "class-in-itself" (i.e., black underclass) unable to become a "class-for-itself" given their embourgeoisement amidst poor material conditions, and the interference of the black bourgeoisie, whose sole aim is to integrate them (i.e., the black underclass), through "traditional" education, into the socioeconomic capitalist power structure against their own interest of obtaining economic gain for its own sake through music, sports, hustling, and illegal activities institutionalized (through education) in the American post-industrial economy and social space by the upper-class of owners and high-level executives servicing the hedonistic desires of a dwindling "multicultural" middle class at home and abroad interested in entertainment provided by black athletes and musicians.

To this end, school for black America in the American post-industrial economic social space is an apparatus concerned with socializing black students for their role as entertainers, i.e., emphasis on athletics, multiculturalism, the arts, social promotion, performance (group work and class presentations), dialogue, etc.; this position is counterbalanced by the initiatives of the black bourgeoisie, which seeks to institutionalize a more prestigious curriculum with emphasis on educating black students for more prestigious service oriented work, i.e., doctors, lawyers, teachers, etc. It should be mentioned that this class struggle between the black bourgeoisie and underclass has characterized black America since their socialization in American capitalist society. One-hundred years ago, this struggle was marked by how best to represent blacks as they transitioned north from an economically deprived agricultural south to a burgeoning industrial north.

NOTES

1. Pierre Bourdieu's (1984) theory of social reproduction refers to several forms of "capital" (cultural, economic, symbolic, and social). I will not go into details about Bourdieu's social reproduction theory, what I will say, however, is that the "capital" references refer to the institutional norms, resources, connections, etc. that one needs in their respective societies' to participate in its cultural, economic, symbolic, and social life. Bourdieu posits that the possession of, for the most part, middle class "capital" is assumed by the educational system in contemporary society, but is not taught. Thus, education theorists (i.e., James Coleman), who have operationalized Bourdieu's concept, conclude, poor students enter school at a disadvantage (i.e., they lack "middle class capital), which leads to their "poor" achievement.

2. To take this position does not make one a racist. For I am not arguing that blacks are genetically inferior, or that race (being black) is the reason they do poorly in school. My argument is that the black community is not a homogenized group with an oppositional ethos to education; instead the community is heterogeneous with members who are more cognitively endowed than others, and speak and comprehend Standard English better than others.

3. In the US Department of Education annual report to congress, *The Condition of Education 2003*, researchers concluded that "[t]he poverty level of students sets the social context for their progress and achievement in school" (U.S. Department of Education, 2003: xi). The report also concluded that "[t]he differences in children's reading skills and knowledge, often observed in later grades, appear to be present when children enter kindergarten and persist or increase throughout the first 2 years of school. For example, [(from the data in their longitudinal study)] when children entered kindergarten (in fall 1998) and after 2 years of school (in spring 2000), White children had higher assessment scores in reading than Black and Hispanic children, and children from poor families had lower scores than children from nonpoor families" (U.S. Department of Education, 2003: iii).

4. This conclusion, I believe, is corroborated by the US Department of Education finding that although "[d]uring kindergarten and 1st grade, children from less advantaged family backgrounds made gains that helped close the gap between themselves and their more advantaged peers in terms of basic reading skills, such as recognizing letters; however, on more difficult skills, such as reading simple words, the gap between these groups widened" (U.S. Department of Education, 2003: iv).

Chapter Three

Where Did Freire Go Wrong? Pedagogy in Globalization: The Grenadian Example

THE GLOBAL PROCESS: THE GRENADIAN EXAMPLE

The case of the black American highlighted in the previous chapter outlines the agential initiatives of black subjects within the dialectics of post-industrial capitalist class relations. This micro-social examination of the failures of black America within post-industrial capitalist social relations in the age of globalization reveals the social structural framework within which black identity gets (over) determined by capital through the politics of education. This chapter looks at this process of cultural and structural homogenization under American ideological hegemony from the global perspective using a particular example, i.e., the Grenadian example.

In today's US dominated "world-economy" or "world-system," the ideological process plays out globally in that to facilitate American policy goals, which amounts to setting the global stage to benefit American multi-national corporations (MNCs), particular models of education have been exported and specific kinds of programs (dealing with manufacturing and low-end service industries) supported financially in developing countries in order to reproduce the role of their citizens, as producers of goods, in the global (American dominated) capitalist economic order. Thus, "results of American policy are rather similar to the British [(the former hegemon of the capitalist world-system)] colonial educational policies of the nineteenth century in that existing metropolitan institutions are exported to the developing areas, often in forms somewhat below domestic standards and sometimes without much adaptation to local conditions" (Altbach, 1995: 455).

In the case of the Caribbean, for example, which has been in America's "backyard" since time immemorial, what we see today under "globalization" is the exportation of an American-style education which emphases the "soft skills" that their (citizens' of the Caribbean) work, i.e., tourism, data-processing, manufacturing, etc., in the new global economy, as dominated by American interest, requires. This undermines and supersedes the struggle of Caribbean people over ideologies or significations that improve their historical conditions. Instead, their identities are commodified and configured within existing configurations of [(economic]) power (Giroux, 1992: 28).

In other words, "The Caribbean enterprise culture . . . is dominated by merchant capital and lacks a sophisticated base in the production and export of modern goods and services" (Watson, 1997: 67).

> Bodies such as the Caribbean Community (CARICOM) . . . and the Association of Caribbean States (ACS) are products and agents of globalization and restructuring. They reflect an unstated recognition that the market and macroeconomic policy coordination are insufficient to produce desired results. They serve or complement a U.S. strategy for deepening the integration of Latin America and the Caribbean into the economy of North America, and more broadly the integration of the entire hemisphere into a single economic bloc [which continues the merchant capital enterprises required by American interest, i.e., tourism and low-end information processing jobs] (66).

The neoliberal logic (i.e., supply side economics) is that the continual growth of these industries or markets will expand the job market, and therefore increase the well being of the masses as capital trickles down from the owners of industry to the "workers and other citizens," who become interpellated consumers and laborers.

In this social environment, as my structural argument implies, the attempt at political, economic diversification (to meet specific needs) or the fashioning of new identities, by the masses, is futile and inconceivable, for the adaptation of the "soft skills" (pedagogical practices), which these industries require, to school curriculums become simply a means of reproducing the social relations of production in the Caribbean, which the global hegemonic economy—American interest—requires. Forcing the Caribbean masses to remain in the post-industrial mode of production one-dimensional laborers (service workers in tourist industry) and consumers dependent on internal and external investors (petit-bourgeois "hybrids" claiming to speak for the masses) from developed countries for all other industries, which their learned skills are ill equipped to tackle. The case of Grenada in the region is most illuminating since the US has had a direct hand in shaping the country for its role in "globalization" or the "world-economy."

GRENADIAN PEDAGOGICAL PRACTICES SINCE INDEPENDENCE

In 1979, five years after their independence, in a bloodless coup spearheaded by Maurice Bishop, the New Jewel Movement in Grenada attempted to reconstitute their society, which was for so-long part of the British colonial (capitalist) heritage. "The socialist program of the Peoples Revolutionary Government (PRG) was optimistic as well as idealistic. Several objectives were framed to thoroughly redevelop the island's economy: (1) construct the Point Salines International Airport to handle wide-bodies jets and invest in the infrastructure necessary for a restructured, locally owned tourism industry; (2) encourage growth of a mixed economy with three major institutional bases—state, cooperative, and private—with the state playing the leading role; (3) improve the standard of living through a comprehensive program aimed at upgrading social services and ensuring basic needs; and (4) diversifying overseas trade and diversifying the portfolio of foreign aid and assistance, particularly courting assistance and link ages with CMEA countries, including Cuba, and improving South-South cooperation" (Conway, 1998: 38).[1]

Consequently,

> . . . the international acclaim that Bishop garnered, championing the antiimperialist cause on behalf of the Nonaligned Movement, was often made at the expense of the Reagan administration. Bishop's rhetoric, like Michael Manley's [(the late Prime Minister of Jamaica at that time)], was answered by U.S. State Department reaction and displeasure. Bishop's principled stances were championed by the U.S. Congressional Black Caucus, but the Republican administration was not amused. In the end, the "Revo" lasted only four years. Strife within the PRG, culminating in a military coup and the assassination of Maurice Bishop and other followers, provided an opportunity for the U.S. military and the Reagan administration to coordinate the invasion and occupation of that Windward "Spice Isle. . . ." Grenada was gradually admitted back into the fold, the airport was finished, tourist facilities were opened to foreign finance, and the national economy was to be open, export-oriented, and dominated by foreign capital (39).

When the People's Revolutionary Government (PRG) led by Maurice Bishop had overthrown the conservative regime of Eric Gairy, "[t]he existing education system matched Grenada's malformed and poorly developed economy (exports of agriculture and agriculture-based products contributed 80 percent or more of total domestic merchandise exports), which was part of its

British colonial (capitalist) heritage. The majority of the population, subsistence peasants and laborers on cocoa, nutmeg, and banana plantations, got a basic level of primary schooling which was often deeply flawed by scant resources, inappropriate curricula, and untrained teachers. A minority of the population went on to elite secondary schools which prepared them for British external school-leaving examinations. Success in these exams gave them entry into 'white collar' jobs in the government service or the small commercial sector, or a better chance to migrate to Britain, the U.S.A., or Trinidad" (Hickling-Hudson, 1988: 10). Those who returned subsequently became the ruling elites ("hybrid" middle class) on the island, looking to England and the U.S.A. for their "ethics."

Under the Bishop administration, work-study, as articulated by the Brazilian educator Freire, "was seen as an educational programme which would help to counter the problem of the abstract, overly theoretical curriculum of the traditional education system. The dichotomy which valued academic subjects and marginalized practical ones was seen as a major weakness of Grenada's colonial type of education system, which had played a part in maintaining the underdevelopment of the economy and the society" (Hickling-Hudson, 1988:11). "The PRG's major aims were to remove the economic stagnation of Gairy's era and to eliminate the dependence syndrome that Grenada had inherited from its colonial past" (De Grauwe, 1991: 338–339). Thus, whereas the former model, under English domination, sought to perpetuate the class privilege and class difference that structured English capitalist society, i.e., the educated who governed in the name of the Queen and the peasants who worked for them, the PRG model, in an attempt to refashion a new identity within a then British dominated capitalist relation of production, introduced a rural-oriented as well as an abstract politically oriented curriculum for building the "economy and improving economic and social welfare of the people" (Coard, 1985: 10, Quoted in De Grauwe, 1991: 339). Educational pedagogy in Grenada during the revolution emphasized agricultural, technical and vocational training "enframed" by a Marxist politically oriented curriculum designed to reconstitute Grenada as a more democratic and socially egalitarian society, a new identity within existing configurations of capitalist—US and British—social relations of power.

After the US invasion in 1983, which brought about the end of the PRG and their programs, the Interim Government supported and directed by the U.S. sought to implement pedagogical practices that aided in the transition of Grenada into the existing global capitalist social relations of production, by paralleling these practices with the export-oriented market economy required by American capitalists: the openness of the national economy, which was then agriculturally dominated, made it susceptible to competition from larger and more global agribusinesses that drove the local markets out of business (the banana industry for example).

The US on account of this, provided foreign direct investment—the U.S. Agency for International Development (USAID) provided more than $120 million in economic assistance from 1984 to 1993. Today, U.S. assistance is channeled primarily through multilateral agencies such as the World Bank—in sectors which could eventually advance to the stage of generating new exports, i.e., tourism and other "service industries in which the need for technical expertise is high and which could be diffused through the rest of the economy, either by the formation of joint ventures or through strategic alliances between local firms and foreign-owned enterprises setting up business in the country."[2]

Thus, whereas the PRG sought to make Grenada self-sufficient, more egalitarian, and independent through the adoption of pedagogical practices that linked work with "banking" study of a new (Marxist) form of social relations, the bureaucrats of the Interim Government under the auspices of the U.S. implemented practices "reoriented toward the world of work" (from an interview with George McGuire, Minister of Education between 1986 and 1990, Quoted in De Grauwe, 1991: 347). This was prescribed to the Grenadians by the global, i.e., U.S., economy (work along technical and vocational lines, and the service industry, i.e., tourism), which perpetuated the dependency and class inequalities of capitalism established by the British. As a consequence, educational pedagogy in Grenada after the revolution and under the auspices of the US, emphasized technical and vocational training, and "soft skills" were promoted at the secondary level "to relieve it from its academic bias and to make it more relevant to the job market" (De Grauwe, 348), i.e., for work in the now dominant service industries, most conspicuously tourism (in the latest IMF statistical assessment of the Grenadian economy, service industries were a substantial contributor to GDP at 68.3 percent in 2000), controlled by foreign markets (see table 2).

This trend continues today, as Grenada is heavily dependent-on and dominated-by foreign capital, which is heavily invested in tourist facilities and all of its accoutrements, i.e., telecommunications, international financial services, etc., which has turned the national economy into an export-oriented low-end service one (Klak et al, 1998). As a result, educational curriculums in Grenada's seventy-six public schools (57 primary and 19 secondary schools) emphasize pedagogical practices—good listener, speaker, writer, dialogue, and cooperative group work, etc.,—which parallel the performance of work in their export-oriented low-end service-dominated economy.[3]

What one finds in Grenada today, which arguably is the norm throughout the developing world within existing configuration of US dominated capitalist power, is an elite, i.e., group of government bureaucrats, who are for the most part foreign trained (educated) in the pragmatics of bourgeois governance, i.e., law, politics, economics, etc., who (as hybrids) serve as middle managers for the protestant bourgeois capitalist class of the developed world, who operate predominantly manufacturing and tourist facilities that employ the masses.

The majority of the masses attend local schools up to the secondary level where they obtain training in the pragmatics of laboring and bourgeois living (i.e., consumerism). They then enter the job market, i.e., tourism, technical work (information-processing), manufacturing, etc., where the sustainable growth of the economy (the expansion and growth of its existing industries) is supposed to reflect in the increase in their real wages, which allows them to exercise the agential moments of bourgeois living or the Protestant ethic and the spirit of capitalism. This has not been the case, however, as capital continues to exploit the labor force, which interpellated as consumers and workers, are unable to obtain either their bare necessities or to exercise their embourgeoisement given their (global) capital determining low wages as a means for accumulating capital or profits from consumers, in predominantly core states, of their export-oriented products: hence, the accumulation of profits from both labor exploitation and the increase of the rate of profit through the consumption of cheaply produced goods by middle class hybrids in core and periphery nations.

Clearly today, then, as the case of Grenada highlights, the dialogical pedagogical practices of post-industrial capitalism, under the auspices of those in power positions (the upper class of owners and high-level executives), cannot be liberating, because it functions as a means of directing (service) labor for the continual benefits of capital.

Hence, dialogue, in this most recent configuration of capitalist social relations of production, essentially, has been incorporated into the "ideological apparatuses" of the power elites, and in the workplace and the classroom it has been "reduced to the act of one person's 'depositing ideas in another, [and has] become a simple exchange of ideas to be 'consumed' by the discussants" (Freire, 2000 [1970]: 89) for their efficient work in either cheap service-labor as in the case of Grenada, or high-end service labor as in the case of black entertainers and athletes in America. In this understanding, the pedagogy of dialogue is unable to foster freedom and simply becomes an enculturative and subjugating mechanism, as opposed to a liberating force, to the existing configurations of power.

Table 3.1.   IMF 2001 Report, Grenada Industries in Percent of GDP 1996–2000 Respectively.

Gross Domestic Product	*100.0*	*100.0*	*100.0*	*100.0*	*100.0*
Primary Sector	9.1	8.5	8.4	8.5	8.2
Agriculture	8.6	8.1	7.9	8.1	7.7
Crops	6.1	5.6	5.4	5.8	5.6
Livestock	0.6	0.6	0.6	0.6	0.5
Forestry	0.4	0.4	0.4	0.3	0.3
Fishing	1.6	1.5	1.5	1.3	1.3
Mining and quarying	0.5	0.5	0.5	0.5	0.5
Secondary Sector	19.6	20.3	21.0	22.2	23.5
Manufacturing	6.7	6.7	7.0	7.3	7.6
Construction	8.0	8.2	9.0	9.6	10.4
Electricity and water	4.8	5.4	5.1	5.3	5.5
Services	71.3	71.2	70.6	69.3	68.3
Wholesale and retail trade	11.5	11.3	11.1	10.9	10.8
Hotels and restaurants	9.5	8.9	8.9	9.4	9.0
Transport and communications	23.3	23.5	24.5	23.2	23.4
Banking and insurance	9.0	9.0	9.5	9.2	9.9
Real estate and housing	4.0	3.8	3.6	3.5	3.4
Government services	17.1	17.9	17.2	17.1	16.4
Other services	2.8	2.8	2.7	2.7	3.2
Less imputed banking charges	5.8	6.1	6.8	6.7	7.8

Source: Central Statistical Office (CSO), Ministry of Finance.

NOTES

1. CMEA—"Council for Mutual Economic Assistance: former trading alliance among state socialist countries, including the Soviet Union, its allies, and Cuba; also abbreviated COMECON" (Klak, 1998: xiii).

2. Rampersad, Frank et al (1997). *Critical Issues in Caribbean Development: The New World Trade Order: Uruguay Round Agreements and Implications for CARICOM States*. Jamaica: Ian Randle Publishers, Pp. 210.

3. Since1996 Grenada's education reform (Basic Education Reform Project) has been the result of its $7.66 million loan from the World Bank. "The Project is designed to improve the quality of basic education, expand access to secondary education, rehabilitate primary and secondary schools facilities, and help curriculum development for primary and secondary schools. The project will close at end-2001, and will be followed by another education project, the OECS Education Reform Project" (IMF 2001 Country Report No. 01/121, 29).

Chapter Four

Toward Democratic Communism: What is to be Done When All are Interpellated and "Embourgeoised" Capitalists

So what is to be done when the aim of those in power position is to interpellate (name) and systemically organize all to benefit capital by giving them (Immanuel Wallerstein's concept of "Embourgeoisement"), through ideological apparatuses such as education, the desires of capital even though the process stratifies social actors along class lines, makes the majority poor, and prevents the latter from dealing critically and creatively with the reality of the social structure given their oppressed relations to the means of production?

This final chapter offers an answer, Democratic Communism, against the anti-economic positions of cosmopolitan liberal thinkers such as Jürgen Habermas and David Held and the identity politics of contemporary education theorists such as Henry Giroux, which make the present capitalist systemic mode of organizing social actors more equitable and liberates those, the poor, who are oppressed by its structural ethic and logic, which they assume to be natural and immutable given their socialization in ideological apparatuses such as education.

THE STRUCTURE/AGENCY PROBLEMATIC

At the level of social and systems integration, this work paints a picture of the local and global social space of our (post) modern or post-industrial era as a mechanical solidarity which is organized around the social ontology of the "Protestant ethic and the spirit of capitalism." This non-agential and oppressive position has sparked great debates in the social scientific literature regarding the constitution of society. A fruitless debate—centered on the nature of human agency within the notion of societal relations as structure, social structure, or system—because the system or structural approach of the social

31

sciences, from Emile Durkheim (1984 [1893]) and Talcott Parsons (1951; 1954; 1977) to Anthony Giddens (1984), Jürgen Habermas (1984 [1981]), and Louis Althusser (2001[1971]), rightly emphasize the suppression of the variability of agential moments in structures-of-signification. This is precisely the aim of the power relations by which society, up till this point in the human archaeological record, is integrated: to suppress the variability of practices, which is an unavoidable element of social being given the potential for the deferment of meaning in ego-centered communicative action, for the underlying norms and values governing the social relational interests of those in power positions, capital since the fourteenth century.

Contrary, to Durkheim's (1984 [1893]) position, and more liberal structural–functionalists like Jürgen Habermas (1984 [1981]), who seek to incorporate the variability of practices as the basis of modern social and systems integration; it is my position that there has yet to be such a solidarity (Organic), only Mechanical ones, as in primitive societies, that attempt to prevent differentiation of values and actions from that of a dominant social structure, by marginalizing differences that undermine the integrative rules of conduct of the social structure. This is a position which also holds true for modern capitalist social relations, for the aim of capital, in their bureaucratic control of the state and economy as the medium for capitalist domination and social integration, is to "mechanically" interpellate and embourgeois social actors (citizens of the state) as laborers for the benefit of the reproduction of surplus-value through the exploitation and marginalization of the bearers of labor power and consumption of their high-end goods and services by a dwindling middle class "embourgeoised" with the wants, needs, and desires of capital.

This interpellation and "embourgeoisement" is done in two ways, either through force and punishment as in the use of military and socio-political force to discipline social actors existing outside of the structuring structure of capitalist social relations to work for capital; or, as highlighted in this work, through ideological discipline, teaching, through ideological state apparatuses such as education, social actors the "ethics" or purposive-rationality needed for both their "ontological security" and the reproduction of the social relation, "practical consciousness," needed by capital to reproduce surplus-value.

The latter Gramscian factor is more problematic than the former and it is within, and out of, such a configuration of power that the means to liberation for labor, one of two subjective positions created by capitalist social relations, must be formulated. In other words, in the former, social movements against military and socio-political force remain vibrant given the overtness by which oppression is attempted and reproduced. So the social actors, given their initial differing "practical consciousness" from that of the forced-upon subjective positions of capitalist social relations, are aware of the very thing that they should be against, and how they should combat it. In the latter, however, the covert, ideological nature by which social and system integration is recursively organized and reproduced makes the oppressed, those who adopt the "ethics" of power, an active participant in their own oppression. For the oppressed recursively organize and reproduce in their practices the purposive-rationality, taken to be, and taught as, the nature of reality and existence as such, that eventually leads to their oppression as workers for investors.

This is precisely what has happened in the dominant post-industrial mode of accumulating surplus value in the contemporary global capitalist world-system. The purposive-rationalities of new and old social movements have been incorporated in the social relations of production to serve capital. Thus, "all" (nations, races, classes, etc.) have been interpellated and embourgeoised by capital in the midst of the ever-increasing proletarianization of the masses, who believe, as a result of their socialization, that their liberation is tied to the success of capital obtaining surplus-value and distributing, "i.e., trickling," it to them through their employment in production and service occupations.

SOCIALIZATION IN POST-INDUSTRIAL CAPITALISM

Although in keeping with the revisionism of Eduard Bernstein (1972 [1961]) I am inclined to agree that liberation for the oppressed, workers, in capitalist social relations is contingent upon the accumulation of wealth, at the social level as opposed to the individual level, i.e., capital; this cannot take place through the "dictatorship of the proletariat," whose consciousness, as my structural determinist approach implies, is that of capital, however, but must be done democratically.

That is, the oppressed, workers, must be raised "from the social position of a proletarian to that of a citizen" (Bernstein, 1972 [1961]: 148). Not a citizen armed solely with the franchise, which dominates capitalist social relations and therefore perpetuates the oppression of the majority, workers, by the minority, capitalists, who represents their will and that of the people through "representative democracy," but a "direct democracy," which offers the opportunity for all to exercise their embourgeoisement as "working capitalists" given their socialization as such. In other words, not a democratization interested solely in, as Max Weber suggests, "leveling of the governed in opposition to the ruling and bureaucratically articulated group," but a democracy true to its denotative meaning: a democracy which in practice means the greatest possible "direct" rule of the *demos* (Weber, 1946: 226). A democracy, in capitalist bourgeois society, organized so that the individual wealth of the few, capitalists, who employ the many, workers, is socially redistributed through taxation by the state controlled by all in a democratic process which "periodically" *selects* and compensates citizen representatives, who, as a result of their compensation for their duty, "ethic of responsibility," in directing the social, is no longer a proletarian, but a middle class agent of "the protestant ethic and the spirit of capitalism."

It is within such a functioning economically democratic determining social space, as opposed through either the liberal cosmopolitanism of David Held (1995, 2004, 2005) and Jürgen Habermas (1996, 1998), or identity politics, which dominate contemporary thought and possess the potentiality to undermine democratic processes, the oppressed will find their liberation.

The former solutions offer either a cosmopolitan democratic polity that will cover the globe (Held, 2004; 2005), or a "democratized regional polity . . . concerned with reinvigorating the democratic capacity to govern in the context of globalization" (Lupel, 2005). Both positions articulate a comprehensive integrated global legal and political system which would provide a 'common structure of action,' protecting people's rights and securing the conditions for the possibility of democratic participation . . ." (Lupel, 2005: 119) in the process of globalization.

The difference between the two is that Jürgen Habermas's position, unlike David Held's "global social democracy," offers a form of regionalism, along the lines of the European Union, as an attempt to incorporate diverse political practices and traditions lost to transnational economic and political actors, while Held "articulates a comprehensive global system of governance (Lupel, 2005: 119). In other words, Habermas proposes a post-Westphalian legal order of cosmopolitan harmonization in which regional polities (like the European Union), global civil society actors, and international organizations such as the UN are committed to human rights and transnational social justice; Held, on the contrary, recommends a global administrative institutional consolidation, a democratic world-polity (Habermas, 1998; Lupel, 2005; Held, 1995, 2005). In either case, the liberal political project, over an economic solution, is stressed as the means of incorporating different provinces of meaning and normative values within the economic (capital) processes of globalization.

This emphasis of achieving an "Organic Solidarity" at the global or regional level to account for the incorporation of diverse political practices and traditions in the process of globalization neglects the fact that identity politics today, stressed through the euphemism of multiculturalism or cosmopolitanism, is the handmaiden of (post-industrial) capital, which offers no liberation for the historical "other" who were and are economically oppressed by capital, but seeks instead to integrate them (hybrid "others"), through legal and social "ideological apparatuses," into its debilitating *post*-colonial and *post*-industrial class stratification.

Be that as it may, just as the position of many critical theorists of education such as Peter McLaren (1988) and Henry Giroux (1992) who "have begun to examine the discursive practices by which student subjectivity (as constructed by race, class, gender, and sexuality) is produced, regulated, and even resisted within the social context of [capitalist] schooling in postindustrial times" (Erevelles, 2000: 25) is a theoretical problematic grounded in their mis-understanding of the dynamics and diachronic effects of the contemporary post-industrial mode of capital accumulation vis-à-vis its relation to the historical "other," the liberal answers posited by Held and Habermas to the global class marginalization accentuated by "globalization" also evade the economic inequality their liberal political model eventually perpetuates.

In other words, the post-structural identitarian analysis of Giroux and McLaren is an attempt to account for the role of subjectivity, as constructed by race, class, gender, and sexuality, within the subjective positions of capitalist domination. As though somehow the former positions are no longer structurally differentiated "classes-in-themselves," but have become discriminating "classes-for-themselves" with distinct discursive practices from those of the subjective positions prescribed by the socioeconomic class relations of the mode of post-industrial capitalist production .

In essence, my argument, in contradistinction to the position of Giroux and McLaren, is that it is only under the auspices of contemporary economic conditions (post-industrial consumerist globality) that they are able to speak of cultural heterogeneity within the existing configuration of capitalist power relations. Globalization or the modern world system is a condition of capitalist bureaucratic organization.

That is to say, the process is simply the continual "expansion" of capitalist discursive practices (mostly American dominated), which as Immanuel Wallerstein points out has always been global in character, across time and space. However, as many globalization theorists of the postmodernist variety have demonstrated (Bell, 1976; Harvey, 1989; Giddens, 1990; Jameson, 1991; Arrighi, 1994; Sklair, 2001; Kellner, 2001), this contemporary condition is no longer characterized or driven by the industrial means for accumulating capital, which dominated the social relations of production of the last one hundred years; instead, the present globalization condition is driven by, post-industrialism (consumerism)—the new means for accumulating capital—, and in such developed society's (like the U.S.), is characterized not by the industrial organization of labor, but rather by capitalist service occupations. So, the rate of economic gain for its own sake or profit has fallen in industrial production due to labor and ecological laws and the crisis of over-accumulated capital from investments in production and trade in developed countries. The practice now is an expansion of industrial production into developing or periphery countries where the rate of labor exploitation has risen given their lack of labor and ecological laws. In the developed hegemonic society, i.e., US, conversely, the economic emphasis is on investment in finance and other future incomes. Thus among governing elites in this interconnected global-institutional frame or social relation of production, the major social emphasis has been participation or integration of historical "others" (i.e., "hybrids") into the existing (financial) configuration of capitalist power relations in order to accumulate profits by servicing the diverse (financial) wants and needs of commodified cultural groups, throughout the globe.

A select few (transnational class), live a "bourgeois" middle and upper middle class lifestyle at the expense of the majority of their workers employed (or not) in out-sourced low-wage service and production jobs controlled by the same owners of these service industries.

In other words, cultural sites, within the logic of the upper-class of owners and high-level executives, become markets to be served by their predestined (capitalist class) "hybrid" representatives, who, working for the upper-class of owners and high-level executives, service their respective "other" community as petit-bourgeois middle class "hybrid" agents of the Protestant ethic who generate profit (surplus-value outside labor exploitation), for capital, through the consumption of cheaply produced (over-priced) products coming out of periphery or developing nations.

No longer is the "other" alienated and marginalized; instead they are embraced and commodified so that the more socialized of their agents can obtain economic gain for its own sake by servicing the "other" poor of their respective communities who are low-wage earners in cheap service and production jobs for capital. So the middle class "other" operating in auxiliary "agents to production"—differentiated service occupations, which capital, to augment cost, contracts out to them—raise the surplus-value through the occupational differentiation produced by capital to increase "the great development of production on a large [(global)] scale and the acceleration of the turnover of industrial capital" (Bernstein, 1972[1961]) amongst the "poor" others" in order to satisfy the (hundred billion dollars a year) consumption needs of the shrinking hybrid middle class "others" working in high-end service industries.

This is why contemporary Freireian pedagogical practices in education as an ideological state apparatus for capital, lack the potential, contrarily to Freire's inference, for liberation as they are utilized to reproduce, in developed countries, the dialogically dominated serviced-oriented social relations of production of post-industrial global capitalism amongst previously discriminated against "others," the majority of whom remain oppressed given their lack of social and economic capital due to the "expansion" of industrial production (i.e., loss of industrial jobs to developing countries) and the rise of labor exploitation in developing countries "serving" the production needs of capital.[1]

Just the same, the liberal political ideologies (global cosmopolitanism and regionalism) proposed by David Held and Jürgen Habermas, given their intent to level *all* for political activism, are reactionary projects intent on making the "other" known through the universalization of their political practices, as opposed to an economic project which challenges the class oppression which the process of globalization seeks to perpetuate. In other words, just as Giroux and McLaren sees the role of constructed identifications within the logic of post-industrial education as somehow revolutionary and anti-establishment even though they actually serve a functional role within this new phase of capital organization and accumulation, the political community proposed by Habermas and Held also binds cosmopolitan identification within the class inequality that constitutes the present globalization process without reevaluating the functional role their 'constitutional patriotism' plays in justifying and legitimizing the very process the content of their models seem to be attacking.

Democratic communism is an alternative model to the identity based liberal matrix of Held and Habermas, which fails to resolve the economic and social woes brought on by the liberal economic process of globalization or the post-industrial financial condition.

WHEN ALL ARE INTERPELLATED AND EMBOURGEOISED CAPITALISTS

Paulo Freire in *Pedagogy of the Oppressed* (2000 [1970]) argues that in modern capitalist society social relations occur between two groups, oppressor and oppressed, or what amounts to the same thing, Marx's capitalist/proletariat classification, and one of the basic elements of the relationship between them is "prescription." "Prescription represents the imposition of one individual's choice upon another, transforming the consciousness of the person prescribed to into one that conforms with the prescriber's consciousness. Thus, the behavior of the oppressed is a prescribed behavior, following as it does the guidelines of the oppressor" (Freire, 2000 [1970]: 47).

For Freire, building on Marx's dialectic, in order for education to serve the oppressed it must be one that emphasizes "the practice of freedom." It must be a pedagogy of the oppressed, which emphasizes their antithetical practical

consciousness as it stands against that of their oppressors; that is, pedagogical techniques that allow for and emphasize democratic dialogue between
practical consciousnesses as opposed to an antidialogical pedagogy in which
the teacher's, as representatives of the oppressors, knowledge is taught to the
student and becomes their (practical) consciousness.

The latter case, the antidialogical scenario (which characterizes the mechanism of the oppressor), is totalitarian, and simply attempts to indoctrinate (in
order to reproduce the dominant social order) rather than liberate, whereas the
former, dialogical pedagogy, allows the oppressed to remain a transformative
agent within their historical material conditions.

Although I agree with Freire that democratic dialogue underscores "the
practice of freedom," I disagree with him and recent critical theorists of education and politics, such as Giroux, McLaren, Held, and Habermas, who, argue within the framework of postmodern and poststructural theorizing, that
this takes place or can take place within existing configurations of capitalist
social relations of power.

Freire's "epistemology is central to his pedagogical principles and method.
He views knowledge as an active process that is made and remade within
changing historical conditions. Following from this is his deeply held belief
that learners must actively create knowledge, not passively absorb donated
information as if it were knowledge" (Hickling-Hudson, 1988: 12).

My take, on the contrary, is that, knowledge is made and remade within a
structure of history (i.e., within the ruling ideas or what amounts to the same
thing, the practices, of those in power position) delimited and integrated by
marginalizing both structurally created differences and structured *différance*,
network of solidarity groups exercising a distinct practical consciousness created through the deferment of meaning in ego-centered communicative action. That is, society, up to this point in the human archaeological record, is
constituted through the contradictory principles of marginality and integration.

Be that as it may, the very necessity of democratic dialogue between subjective positions paradoxically requires the practice of "banking education."
For the structure of the democratic process necessitates a differing social structure from that of the existing configuration of capitalist social relations of
power, which necessarily engenders inequality and gives rise to the oppressor/
oppressed social relationship through the creation and exploitation of labor.
In other words, in order to facilitate egalitarian democratic dialogue between
subjective positions of the life-world, the historical capitalist structure of signification and its ideological apparatuses must be supplanted by democratic
ones with "ideological apparatuses" intent on naming and socializing social
actors for democratic social relations.[2]

So in essence, the argument here is that it is not the pedagogical practices in and of themselves, as they stand in dialectical opposition to those utilized by power, that are the locus of causality for democratic change, as Freire postulates. On the contrary, it is the social ontology within which they are incorporated, which is problematic. In other words, my conclusion, as it relates to Freire's Manichean polarity, is that the proletariat or oppressed consciousness in dialogue[3] will never be allowed to reveal an action-theoretic pedagogy distinct from the oppressor consciousness if it functions within existing configurations of capitalist power; for structurally speaking, both the consciousness of the oppressor and oppressed are structured, differentially related, within a metaphysical ontology justified as universal and objective based on the "technical rationality" of the oppressor as it is delimited by the material conditions of the oppressed.[4] This implies, as in the Hegelian master/slave dialectic, that the oppressor needs the oppressed to remain in their conditions so that they may exercise their "oppressor" practical consciousness. Hence, it is not based on what is already understood that the economically oppressed will find their liberation as Habermas and Held attempt to do with their extrapolation of democratic liberalism on a regional and global scale. Instead, the key to liberation lies in either: 1) the undemocratic "dictatorship of the proletariat" through revolutionary minded intellectual elites, as argued by Vladimir Lenin; 2) or in a new governing social system, instituted by these elites, which is more democratic than the liberal/conservative matrix which contemporarily dominates globalization or the modern world-system.

In the former approach, the idea is that the revolutionary minded intellectual elites in control of state ideological apparatuses must prescribe (by gaining control of state ideological apparatuses), contrary to Freire, a consciousness *for* and *with* the oppressed (against their "semi-intransitive consciousness") so that they may recursively reproduce—in the form of society—a democratic form of being-in-the-world that will allow them to participate in their world as they encounter it. For initially, according to this premise, what human identity the oppressed have, as Antonio Gramsci so eloquently observed, "is given to them only as members of an inclusive corporate body—the collective worker, or integral society, or, at the apex, the State." If left alone, "[t]he ordinary mass of people can think nothing, do nothing and be nothing without the intercession of the intellectual elite. It feels, but does not understand; it has a spontaneous character, but no consciousness; activity, but no awareness; it comprehends through faith not reason, so that didactically the only means of reaching it is through the endless repetition of the same message wrapped in different coverings. Its province is the folklore of philosophy, no more than common sense laced with religion. The mass, it would seem, has the same limited comprehension as Aristotle's slave [;] the same qualities of loyalty and discipline and the same incapacity to function as an autonomous being" (Harding, 1997: 212).

The latter approach also assumes the underlining social character of consciousness. However, unlike Habermas and Held who seem to neglect the fact that their models (democratic dialogue within the class marginalization of globalism) perpetuate the very thing, global inequality perpetuated by global capitalism, they are against, my assumption is "enframed" in an historical understanding that bears witness to the invariable nature of the ideology of bourgeois domination once internalized by all social actors.

Thus, the premise here is not that the oppressed be taught an underlying ontology that diametrically opposes the capitalist social structure, which gives rise to their oppression and their initial consciousness. On the contrary, the understanding here is that the majority of the oppressed, once interpellated and integrated into the social dynamics of the capitalist social structure, assumes it's pragmatic labor ethic or practical consciousness, which is equated with the nature of reality and existence as such in spite of the class stratification and alienation that it brings about. So logically, the question which arises as a result of this structure determining social action and consciousness is: what is to be done ethically, by the revolutionary minded intellectual elites, when all are interpellated and believing capitalists who solely seek economic gain so that they may avoid the pitfalls of poverty and live the good life or raise their standard of living?

The answer, democratic communism, I propose does not require the proposed revolutionary reconfiguration of the capitalist social space, which dominated for so long Marxist or left leaning thought. This is a final consideration, which must be taken into account when capital refuses to implement political institutions that govern the economic for social, as opposed to class or individual, benefits. That is, capital, in control of the state and its apparatuses, refuses to allow for the (re) construction of democratic institutions that "disembeds" the economic from the political, and makes the latter the means to the acquisition of the good life as opposed to solely economic aid or welfare.

My position, conversely, is that the political or the liberal bourgeois understanding of democracy should be re-conceptualized and reconfigured by the revolutionary-minded intellectuals in order to account for the "embourgeoisement" of the masses. For it is through the political that bourgeois ideological domination, which insists on preventing the "embourgeoised" masses from obtaining the good life given labor laws intended on helping capital increase profits, gets institutionalized. So the political reconfiguration I am suggesting implies that not just the capitalists (with capital) direct the political for the "ultimate ethical end" of economic gain for its own sake, but those interpellated and embourgeoised with the wants, desires, and needs of capital also participate in the process.

That is, the liberal representative "leadership" democracy with paid officials *elected* by "rational" social actors, which contemporarily dominate capitalist social structures and is supported by Held and Habermas, should be supplanted with a direct democracy with paid citizens representing their "own" interests.

What this global "leaderless" democracy would resemble is an American type republic in every nation-state governed not by *elected* officials (with the exception of the Presidential position) solely interested in "politics as a vocation" for the "ultimate ethical end" of economic gain for its own sake by any means necessary, but by a congress comprised of salaried representatives renewed every three to four years with other citizens *selected* randomly from the masses (as in the American jury system) to serve the social structure, which is global in nature, through an "ethic of responsibility" aimed toward the "ultimate ethical end" of justice (economic, social and political) for "all." In this understanding, the populous directly represent their (social and political) interests within their own nation-states, and the (economic) wealth of the (global) social structure is socially redistributed through salary and health compensation obtained from taxation, loans, aid, etc., which makes the system socially, politically, and economically democratic: hence, democratic association (communism) implemented on the social organization of capitalism.

In other words, the means of production remains the property of individual capitalists, who continue "to appropriate to themselves the results of the production" (Bernstein, 1972 [1961]: 19), but the social process of production is no longer suppressed but becomes redistributed through the political; that means, the working classes, as they participate in the political process as *selected* officials called upon to serve the state, are elevated "from the social position of a proletarian to that of a citizen" (Bernstein, 1972 [1961]: 148) benefiting from, defending, and directing, the social wealth produced by their labor and the ingenuity of the capitalist class through their participation in the political process as "*selected*" officials representing—no longer marginalized—diverse views and interests arrived at through the deferment of meaning in ego-centered communicative action.

NOTES

1. My reading of globalization completely breaks away from critical social theorists (Gilder 1989, 2000; Kaku, 1997; Kellner), who see globalization as an integral part of the scientific and technological revolutions of the modern era. I believe it is

not necessarily the case that the scientific and technological revolutions of the modern era should give rise to present global processes; in fact, the networking of people, ideas, forms of culture, and people across national boundaries has been an integral aspect of human culture. So much so, that I would venture to call it a natural process. Thus, for me, "modern" globalization is a movement whereby a dominant culture, i.e., bourgeois capitalist culture of the West (America and Western Europe), attempts to reproduce its way of life by integrating the world's population into its structures of signification, i.e., freedom, democracy, increased wealth, and happiness (the protestant ethic). All of this is accomplished through a set of social relations directed and controlled by the market, military power, and supervisory institutions such as the U.N.

2. This position diametrically opposes that of postmodernist critical theorists of education, who, building on Freire, push for a democratic dialogical pedagogy within the structure of existing configuration of capitalist power. My position, which builds on the work of Herbert Marcuse (1964), doubts the potential of dialogue (outside of intellectual indoctrination or guidance), within current existing configurations of power, to liberate the oppressed. That is, I believe, in terms of the constitution of contemporary society, capitalist domination, and its discourse Protestantism, has been sustained through the appeal to reason, and that this "technical rationality," which dominates the capitalist normative world, and makes it appear to be natural (ideology), makes life for both oppressed and oppressor an objective reality in which shortcomings are more a product of individual failure than that of the social (objective) reality. Thus, dialogical pedagogy within this existing configuration of power becomes rhetorical, the means (forcefully or otherwise) of persuading those who do not share in capitalist discursive practices to do so, since structurally an "other" form of being in the world only serves to differentially delimit the existing configuration of power.

3. This characteristic of the American capitalist social structure, defined in relation to "other" forms of being-in-the-world, and the attempt by its ruling elites to globally institutionalize their ethos, speaks to the illusion of reifying thought—"the idea," as Habermas observes, "that the differentiation of an objective world means totally excluding the social and the subjective worlds from the domains of rationally motivated agreement" (1984 [1981]: 73).

In such a reality, democratic dialogue is a means of surviving or coping (therapy in essence), which takes the place of morality in the Nietszchean sense, within the objective reality. That is, the dialogue in which the oppressed partakes, accentuates their subjective position as an "other," and therefore releases the objective reality from any faults in creating that position—subsequently making these thoughts and their practices antithetical (delimiting) ideas. In which case, these thoughts or ideas, that is, thoughts of the oppressed as expressed in dialogue within the capitalist social structure, become simply predefined lexicons and representations of signification within the objective reality that are already incorporated in its logic (they structurally delimit the dominant order) to disprove their possibilities by being labeled irrational, utopic, or simply "other"—hence substantiating the position of the capitalist order or culture through its perceived rationality and success, and in doing so justifying the conditions of the oppressed, i.e., marginalized commodified "others," who delimit the social relations of production of the existing configuration of power.

4. In fact, the way I see it, Freire's failure (the failure of his model, i.e., the integration of work and study to reconstitute society), that is, its failure in its implementation in the Grenadian revolution, lies in his under estimation of the power of modern society's emphasis on "technical rationality," as the defining element of its institutions (education in this case), to serve as an all encompassing "ideological apparatus" which incorporates even the pedagogy of the oppressed itself to serve as a mechanism of control. Rationality, in this understanding, serves to fashion the society into a Durkheimian Mechanical Solidarity as opposed to an Organic one.

In other words, it would be one thing if the structure of the institutions were the problem, as Freire alludes to. But in modernity the institutions themselves are not the problem, as many postmodernists have pointed out; rather it is the universal truth claim that the appeal to reason casts over these institutions (to validate their existence), which makes them "ideological apparatuses" in which contradictory thoughts, such as those of the oppressed, are incorporated in the logic of the system to serve as a mechanism of control by demonstrating their irrationalities and absurdities. In this sense, "the worldview . . . does not permit differentiation between the world of existing states of affairs, valid norms and expressible subjective experiences. The linguistic worldview is reified as the world order and cannot be seen as an interpretive system open to criticism. Within such a system of orientation, actions cannot reach that critical zone in which communicatively achieved agreement depends upon autonomous yes/no responses to criticizable validity claims" (Habermas, 1984 [1981]: 71).

References

Adorno, Theodor W. (2000 [1966]). *Negative Dialectics*. New York: Continuum.

Allen, Richard L. (2001). *The Concept of Self: A Study of Black Identity and Self Esteem*. Detroit: Wayne State University Press.

Altbach, Philip G. (1995 [1971]). "Education and Neocolonialism." Pp. 452–456 in *The Post-colonial Studies Reader*, edited by Bill Ashcroft et al. London and New York: Routledge.

Althusser, Louis (2001 [9171]). *Lenin and Philosophy and Other Essays*. New York: Monthly Review Press.

Altschuler, Richard (ed.) (1998). *The living Legacy of Marx, Durkheim, and Weber: Applications and Analyses of Classical Sociological Theory By Modern Social Scientists*. New York: Gordian Knot Books.

Arrighi, Giovanni (1994). *The Long Twentieth Century*. London: Verso.

Asante, Molefi Kete (1988). *Afrocentricity*. New Jersey: Africa World.

Asante, Molefi K. (1990). *Kemet, Afrocentricity and Knowledge*. New Jersey: Africa World.

Asante, Molefi K. (1990). "African Elements in African-American English." Pp. 19–33, in *Africanisms in American Culture*, Edited by Joseph E. Holloway. Bloomington and Indianapolis: Indiana University Press.

Balibar, Etienne and Immanuel Wallerstein (1991). *Race, Nation, Class: Ambiguous Identities*. London and New York: Verso.

Ballantine, Jeanne, H. (1993). *The Sociology of Education: A systematic Analysis* (3rd Edition). New Jersey: Prentice Hall.

Bankston, Carl L. and Stephen J. Caldas (1996). "Majority Black Schools and the Perpetuation of Social Injustice: the Influence of De facto Segregation on Academic Achievement." *Social Forces*, 75, 535–555.

Bell, Daniel (1976). *The Coming of Post-Industrial Society*. New York: Basic Books.

Bergin, David and Helen Cooks (2002). "High School Students of Color Talk About Accusations of 'Acting White.'" *The Urban Review* 34: 113–134.

Bhabha, Homi (1995). "Cultural Diversity and Cultural Differences," Pp. 206–209. In *The Post-colonial Studies Reader*, Eds. Bill Ashcroft et al. London and New York: Routledge.

Blassingame, John W. (1972). *The Slave Community: Plantation Life in the Antebellum South*. New York: Oxford University Press.

Bourdieu, Pierre (1990 [1980]). *The Logic of Practice* (Richard Nice, Trans.). Stanford, California: Stanford University Press.

Bourdieu, Pierre (1984). *Distinction: A Social Critique of the Judgement of Taste*. Massachusetts: Harvard University Press.

Boswell, Terry (1989). "Colonial Empires and the Capitalist World-Economy: A Time Series Analysis of Colonization, 1640–1960." *American Sociological Review*, 54, 180–196.

Bowles, Samuel and Herbert Gintis (1976). *Schooling in Capitalist America: Educational Reform and the Contradictions of Economic Life*. New York: Basic Books.

Braverman, Harry (1998 [1974]. *Labor and Monopoly Capital: The Degradation of Work in the Twentieth Century*. New York: Monthly Review Press.

Brecher, Jeremy and Tim Costello (1998). *Global Village or Global Pillage: Economic Reconstruction from the bottom up* (2nd ed.). Cambridge, Mass.: South End Press.

Caws, Peter (1997). *Structuralism: A Philosophy for the Human Sciences*. New York: Humanity Books.

Chase-Dunn, Christopher (1975). "The effects of international economic dependence on development and inequality: A cross-national study." *American Sociological Review*, 40, 720–738.

Chase-Dunn, Christopher and Richard Rubinson (1977). "Toward a Structural Perspective on the World-System." *Politics & Society*, 7,4: 453–476.

Clark, Robert P. (1997). *The Global Imperative: An Interpretive History of the Spread of Humankind*. Boulder, Colorado: Westview Press.

Coleman, James S. (1988). "'Social Capital' and Schools." Education Digest 53 (8): 69.

Coser, Lewis (1956). *The Functions of Social Conflict*. New York: The Free Press.

Covino, William A. and David A. Jolliffe (1995). *Rhetoric: Concepts, Definitions, Boundaries*. Needham Heights, Massachusetts: Allyn and Bacon.

Culler, Jonathan (1976). *Saussure*. Great Britain: Fontana/Collins.

Dahrendorf, Ralf (1959). *Class and Class Conflict in Industrial Society*. California: Stanford University Press.

De Grauwe, Anton (1991). "Education and Political Change: The Case of Grenada (1979–89)." *Comparative Education* 27, 3, 335–356.

Domhoff, William G. (2002). *Who Rules America? Power & Politics* (Fourth Edition). Boston: McGraw Hill.

Drake, St. Claire (1965). "The Social and Economic Status of the Negro in the United States," Pp. 3–46. In *The Negro American*, Edited by Talcott Parsons and Kenneth B. Clark. Boston: Houghton Mifflin Company.

Dreeben, Robert and Rebecca Barr (1983). *How Schools Work*. Chicago: University of Chicago Press.

Durkheim, Emile (1984 [1893]). *The Division of Labor in Society* (W.D. Halls, Trans.). New York: The Free Press.

Eagleton, Terry (1991). *Ideology: An Introduction.* London: Verso.

Edgar, Andrew and Peter Sedgwick (Eds.) (1999). *Key Concepts in Cultural Theory.* London: Routledge.

Elkins, Stanley (1959). *Slavery: A Problem in American Institutional and Intellectual Life.* Chicago: University of Chicago Press.

Engels, Frederick (2000 [1884]. *The Origin of the Family, Private Property, and the State.* New York: Pathfinder Press.

Erevelles, Nirmala (2000). "Educating Unruly Bodies: Critical Pedagogy, Disability Studies, and the Politics of Schooling." *Educational Theory* 50, 1, Pp. 25–

Fanon, Frantz (1967 [1952]). *Black Skin, White Masks* (Charles Lam Markmann, Trans.). New York: Grove Press.

Florida Department of Education. (2004). Understanding *FCAT Reports 2005.* Retrieved February 15, 2005 from www.fldoe.org/news/.

Florida Department of Education. (2005). *Governor's Press Release:2005 FCAT Reading and Mathematics.* Retrieved February 15, 2005 from www.fldoe.org/news/.

Florida Department of Education. (2005). *Governor Bush and Commissioner Winn Announce FCAT Results for 3rd and 12th Grade.* Retrieved February 15, 2005 from www.fldoe.org/news/.

Florida Department of Education. (2005). *Governor Bush and Commissioner Winn Announce FCAT Reading and Mathematics Results for Grades 3 Through 10.* Retrieved February 15, 2005 from www.fldoe.org/news/.

Florida Department of Education. (2005). *Reading Scores Statewide Comparison for 2001 to 2005.* Retrieved February 15, 2005 from www.fldoe.org/news/.

Florida Department of Education. (2005). *FCAT Reading and Mathematics Results for Grades 3 through 10.* . Retrieved May 12, 2004 from www.fldoe.org/news/.

Florida Department of Education. (2005). FCAT *Sunshine State Standards District Report of Schools.* Retrieved May 12, 2004 from www.fldoe.org/news/.

Florida Department of Education. (2005). FCAT *Reading Students at Achievement Level 1: Grades 3–10.* Retrieved May 12, 2004 from www.fldoe.org/news/.

Ford, Donna Y. and J. John Harris (1996). "Perceptions and Attitudes of Black Students Toward School, Achievement, and Other Educational Variables." *Child Development* 67: 1141–1152.

Fordham, Signithia and John Ogbu (1986). "Black Students' School Success: Coping With the Burden of 'Acting White.'" *Urban Review* 18, 176–206.

Foucault, Michel (1977 [1975]). *Discipline and Punish: The Birth of the Prison* (Alan Sheridan, Trans.). London: Penguin Books.

Frazier, Franklin E. (1939). *The Negro Family in America.* Chicago: University of Chicago Press.

Frazier, Franklin E. (1957). *Black Bourgeoisie: The Rise of a New Middle Class.* New York: The Free Press.

Freire, Paulo (1973). *Education for Critical Consciousness.* New York: Herder & Herder.

Freire, Paulo (2000 [1970]). *Pedagogy of the oppressed*. Translated by Myra Bergman Ramos. New York: Continuum.

Genovese, Eugene (1974). *Roll, Jordan, Roll*. New York: Pantheon Books.

Giddens, Anthony (1984). The Constitution of Society: Outline of the Theory of Structuration. Cambridge: Polity Press.

Giddens, Anthony (1990). *Consequences of Modernity*. England: Polity Press.

Gilder, George (1989). *Microcosm*. New York: Simon and Schuster.

Gilder, George (2000). *Telecosm*. New York: Simon and Schuster.

Giroux, Henry (1992). *Border Crossings: Cultural Workers and the Politics of Education*. New York: Routledge.

Giroux, Henry and Peter McLaren (Eds.) (1994). *Between Borders: Pedagogy and the Politics of Cultural Studies*. New York and London: Routledge.

Glazer, Nathan and Daniel P. Moynihan (1963). *Beyond the Melting Pot*. Cambridge: Harvard University Press.

Gramsci, Antonio (1978). *Selections from Prison Notebooks*, edited by Q. Hoare and G.N. Smith. London: Lawrence and Wishart.

Gutman, Herbert (1976). *The Black Family in Slavery and Freedom 1750–1925*. New York: Pantheon Books.

Habermas, Jürgen (1984 [1981]). *The Theory of Communicative Action: Reason and the Rationalization of Society* (volume 1). Translated by Thomas McCarthy. Boston: Beacon Press.

Habermas, Jürgen (1987 [1981]). *The Theory of Communicative Action: Lifeworld and System: A Critique of Functionalist Reason* (Volume 2, Thomas McCarthy, Trans.). Boston: Beacon Press.

Hare, Nathan (1965 [1991]). *The Black Anglo-Saxons*. Chicago: Third World Press.

Harding, Neil (1997). "Intellectuals and Socialism: Making and Breaking the Proletariat." Pp. 195–222 in *Intellectuals in Politics: From the Dreyfus Affair to Salman Rushdie*, edited by Jeremy Jennings and Anthony Kemp-Welch. London: Routledge.

Harris, Marvin. (1999). *Theories of Culture in Postmodern Times*. Walnut California: AltaMira Press.

Harvey, David (1989). *The Condition of Postmodernity*. Cambridge, MA: Blackwell.

Herskovits, Melville J. (1958 [1941]). *The Myth of the Negro Past*. Boston: Beacon Press.

Hegel, G.W.F. (1977 [1807]). *Phenomenology of Spirit* (A.V. Miller, Trans.). Oxford: Oxford University Press.

Hickling-Hudson, Anne (1988). "Toward Communication Praxis: Reflections on the Pedagogy of Paulo Freire and Educational Change in Grenada." *Journal of Education* 170, 2, Pp. 9–38.

Holloway, Joseph E. (ed.) (1990). *Africanisms in American Culture*. Bloomington and Indianapolis: Indiana University Press.

Horkheimer, Max and Theodor W. Adorno (2000 [1944]. *Dialectic of Enlightenment* (John Cumming, Trans.). New York: Continuum.

Horvat, Erin M. and Kristine S. Lewis (2003). "Reassessing the "Burden of 'Acting White'": The Importance of Peer Groups in Managing Academic Success." *Sociology of Education* 76, 265–280.

House, James S. (1977). "The Three Faces of Social Psychology." *Sociometry* 40: 161 177.

House, James S. (1981). "Social Structure and Personality." Pp. 525–561 in *Sociological Perspectives on Social Psychology*, edited by Morris Rosenberg and Ralph Turner. New York: Basic Books.

Huntington, Samuel P. (1996). *The Clash of Civilizations and the Remaking of World Order*. New York: Simon and Schuster.

Inkeles, Alex (1959). "Personality and Social Structure." Pp. 249–276 in *Sociology Today*, edited by Robert K. Merton, Leonard Broom, and Leonard S. Cottrell, Jr. New York: Basic Books.

Inkeles, Alex (1960). "Industrial man: The Relation of Status, Experience, and Value." *American Journal of Sociology* 66: 1–31.

Inkeles, Alex (1969). "Making Men Modern: On the causes and consequences of individual change in six developing countries." *American Journal of Sociology* 75: 208–225.

Jameson, Fredric (1991). *Postmodernism, or the Cultural Logic of Late Capitalism*. Durham, NC: Duke University Press.

Jameson, Fredric and Masao Miyoshi (Eds.) (1998). *The cultures of globalization*. Durham: Duke University Press.

JanMohamed, Abdul R. (1994). "Some Implications of Paulo Freire's Border Pedagogy." Pp. 242–252. *In Between Borders: Pedagogy and the Politics of Cultural Studies*, Edited by Henry A. Giroux and Peter McLaren. New York and London: Routledge.

Kaku, Michio (1997). *Visions: How Science Will Revolutionize the 21st Century*. New York: Anchor Books.

Karenga, Maulana (1993). *Introduction to Black Studies*. California: The University of Sankore Press.

Kellner, Douglas (2002). "Theorizing Globalization." Sociological Theory 20, 3: 285–305.

Klak, Thomas (1998). *Globalization and Neoliberalism: The Caribbean Context*. Lanham, Maryland: Rowman & Littlefield Publishers, Inc.

Kneller, George F. (1964). *Introduction to the Philosophy of Education*. New York: John Wiley & Sons, Inc.

Labov, William (1972). *Language in the Inner-City: Studies in the Black English Vernacular*. Philadelphia: University of Pennsylvania Press.

Levine, Lawrence W. (1977). *Black Culture and Black Consciousness: Afro-American Folk Thought from Slavery to Freedom*. New York: Oxford University Press.

Lévi-Strauss, Claude (1963). *Structural Anthropology* (Claire Jacobson and Brooke Schoepf, Trans.). New York: Basic Books.

Lyman, Stanford M. and Arthur J. Vidich (1985). *American Sociology: Worldly Rejections of Religion and Their Directions*. New Haven and London: Yale University Press.

Marcuse, Herbert (1964). *One-Dimensional Man*. Boston: Beacon Press.

Marshall, Gordon (1998). *A Dictionary of Sociology*. New York: Oxford University Press.

Marx, Karl and Friedrich Engels (1964). *The Communist Manifesto*. London, England: Penguin Books.

Marx, Karl (1992). *Capital: A Critique of Political Economy* (Volume 1). Translated from the third German edition by Samuel Moore and Edward Aveling. New York: International Publishers.

McLaren, Peter (1988). "Schooling the Postmodern Body: Critical Pedagogy and the Politics of Enfleshment." Journal of Education 170, 1: 53–83.

McMichael, Philip (1996). "Globalization: Myths and Realities." *Rural Sociology* 61 (1): 274–291.

Mocombe, Paul (2001). *A Labor Approach to the Development of the Self or "Modern Personality": The Case of Public Education*. Thesis Florida Atlantic University. Ann Arbor: UMI.

Moynihan, Daniel P. (1965). *The Negro Family*. Washington, D.C.: Office of Planning and Research, US Department of Labor.

Murray, Charles (1984). *Losing Ground: American Social Policy 1950–1980*. New York: Basic Books.

Myrdal, Gunnar (1944). *An American Dilemma: The Negro Problem and Modern Democracy*. New York: Harper & Row Publishers.

Ogbu, John U. (1974). *The Next Generation*. New York: Academic Press.

Ogbu, John U. (1990). "Minority Education in Comparative Perspective." *Journal of Negro Education*, 59, 45–57.

Ogbu, John U. (1991). "Low School Performance as an Adaptation: The Case of Blacks in Stockton, California." Pp. 129–86 in *Minority Status and Schooling: A Comparative Study of Immigrant and Involuntary Minorities*, edited by Margaret Gibson and John U. Ogbu. New York: Garland Press.

Ortner, Sherry (1984). "Theory in Anthropology Since the Sixties," *Comparative Studies in Society and History* 26: 126–66.

Orr, Amy J. (2003). "Black-White Differences in Achievement: The Importance of Wealth." *Sociology of Education* 76, 281–304.

Portes, Alejandro (1997). "Neoliberalism and the Sociology of Development: Emerging Trends and Unanticipated Facts." *Population and Development Review* 23 (2): 353–372.

Roszak, Theodore (1972). *Where the Wasteland Ends*. London: Faber & Faber.

Runkle, Gerald (1968). *A History of Western Political Theory*. New York: The Ronald Press Company.

Said, Edward (1979 [1978]). *Orientalism*. New York: Vintage Books.

Schwalbe, Michael L. (1993). "Goffman Against Postmodernism: Emotion and the Reality of the Self." *Symbolic Interaction* 16(4): 333–350.

Saussure de, Ferdinand (1986 [1916]). *Course in General Linguistics*. Chicago: Open Court.

Sennett, Richard (1998). *The Corrosion of Character.* New York: W.W. Norton & Company.

Sklair, Leslie (1995). *Sociology of the Global System.* Baltimore: Westview Press.

Sklair, Leslie (2001). *The Transnational Capitalist Class*. Cambridge: Blackwell.

Slemon, Stephen (1995). "The Scramble for Post-colonialism," Pp. 45–52. In *The Post-colonial Studies Reader*, Eds. Bill Ashcroft et al. London and New York: Routledge.

Smith, Vicki (1998). "Employee Involvement, Involved Employees: Participative Work Arrangements in a White-Collar Service Occupation." Pp. 460–473 in *Working in America: Continuity, Conflict, and Change*, edited by Amy S. Wharton. California: Mayfield Publishing Company.

Sowell, Thomas (1975). *Race and Economics*. New York: David McKay.

Sowell, Thomas (1981). *Ethnic America*. New York: Basic Books.

Spring, Joel (1994). *American Education*, (6th edition). New York: McGraw-Hill.

Stampp, Kenneth (1956 [1967]). *The Peculiar Institution*. New York: Alfred Knopf, Inc.

Sturrock, John (ed.) (1979). *Structuralism and Since: From Lévi-Strauss to Derrida*. Oxford: Oxford University Press.

Sudarkasa, Niara (1980). "African and Afro-American Family Structure: A Comparison," The *Black Scholar*, 11: 37–60.

Sudarkasa, Niara 91981). "Interpreting the African Heritage in Afro-American Family Organization." In Black Families," Ed. Harriette P. McAdoo. California: Sage Publications.

Turner, Ralph H. (1976). "The Real Self: From Institution to Impulse." *American Journal of Sociology* 81: 989–1016.

Turner, Ralph H. (1988). "Personality in Society: Social Psychology's Contribution to Sociology." *Social Psychology Quarterly* 51; 1: 1–10.

Tye, Kenneth (1999). *Global Education: A Worldwide Movement*. California: Interdependence Press.

Tyson, Karolyn (2003). "Notes from the Back of the Room: Problems and Paradoxes in the Schooling of Young Black Students." *Sociology of Education* 76, 326–343.

Tyson, Karolyn et al (2005). "It's Not 'a Black Thing': Understanding the Burden of Acting White and Other Dilemmas of High Achievement." *American Sociological Review* 70, 582–605.

U.S. Department of Education (2003). *The Condition of Education 2003*, NCES 2003 067. Washington, DC.

Van Hook, Jennifer (2002). "Immigration and African American Educational Opportunity: The Transformation of Minority Schools." *Sociology of Education*, 75, 169–189.

Wallerstein, Immanuel (1974). *The Modern World-System*. New York and London: Academic Press.

Wallerstein, Immanuel (1982). "The Rise and Future Demise of the World Capitalist System: Concepts for Comparative Analysis," Pp. 29–53. *In Introduction to the Sociology of "Developing Societies*," Eds. Hamza Alavi and Teodor Shanin. New York: Monthly Review Press.

Watkins, S. Craig (1998). *Representing: Hip-Hop Culture and the Production of Black Cinema*. Chicago: The University of Chicago Press.

Weber, Max (1958 [1976]. *The Protestant Ethic and The Spirit of Capitalism*. New York: Charles Scribner's Sons.

Wilson, William J. (1978). *The Declining Significance of Race: Blacks and Changing American Institutions*. Chicago and London: The University of Chicago Press.

Wilson, William J. (1987). *The Truly Disadvantaged*. Chicago and London: University of Chicago Press.

Wilson, William J. (1998). "The Role of the Environment in the Black-White Test Score Gap." Pp. 501–510 in *The Black-White Test Score Gap*, edited by Christopher Jencks and Meredith Phillips. Washington, DC: Brookings Institution Press.

Woodson, Carter G. (1933 [1969]). *The Mis-Education of the Negro*. Washington: Associated Publishers Inc. Young, Iris Marion (1994). "Gender as Seriality: Thinking about Women as a Social Collective," *Signs* 19: 713–738.

Zeitlin, Irving M. (1990). *Ideology and the development of sociological theory* (4th ed.). Englewood Cliffs, New Jersey: Prentice-Hall.

Index

Altbach, Philip G. (1995), 45
Althusser, Louis (2001 [1971]), ix, 4, 32, 45
American Blacks: as agents of capitalist social structure, 15; black children, educational failure of, 15–17, 18–19, 22n4; Black English Vernacular, 17, 18, 19, 20, 21; "burden of acting white", 16, 18, 19; capitalist education and, 16–17, 21–22; "embourgeoisement" of, 15, 21; Florida Comprehensive Assessment Test and, 20; framing the problem of, 17–20; indigent structural position of, 15–16; pathological-pathogenic dialect of, 20, 21; Protestant ethic and, 15; sociolinguistics and, 18–21; "Standard English" and, 16, 18, 20; status groups of, 15; test taking and, 15, 16, 17, 19; William Labov on, 17–18
American capitalist society, restructuring of, 10–11
American policy goals and education, 23
Arrighi, Giovanni (1994), 6, 35, 45
Association of Caribbean States (ACS), 24

"banking education", 38
Bankston, Carl L. and Stephen J. Caldas, (1996), 17, 45
Being in capitalism, 11–12, 42n3
Bell, Daniel (1976), 6, 35, 45
Bergin, David and Helen Cooks (2002), 19, 45
Bernstein, Eduard (1972 [1961]), 33, 36, 41
Bishop, Maurice, 25
Black English Vernacular (BEV), 17, 18, 19, 20, 21
Bourdieu, Pierre (1973), 1, 15, 22n1
bourgeois capitalist class: definition of, 1; diagram representing structure of its culture, 5; effect on education, 1, 2; effect on selves, 1; ideological domination institutionalized, 40; imposition of their will, 1
Bowles, Samuel and Herbert Gintis (1976), 1, 46
Braverman, Harry (1998), 9, 10, 46

capitalism: aim of industrial capitalism, 11; aim of post-industrialism capitalism, 11–12; *Being* in, 11–12, 13n3; Caribbean enterprise culture and, 24; direct democracy and, 33–34;

interpellating/embourgeois of social
actors and, 32–33, 40–41;
pedagogical curriculum reform
movements and, 11–12; role of
subcultures in, 9; scientific
management movement and, 9–10;
socialization in post-industrial, 33–37;
socialization of *Being* in, 11–12,
13n3. *See also* spirit of capitalism
capitalist ideological domination, 3–4
Caribbean Community (CARICOM), 24
Caribbean nations, supply side
economics and, 24
causality for democratic change, 39
Chase-Dunn, Christopher (1977), viii, 3,
46
Coleman, James (1988), 19, 46
constitutional patriotism, 37
consumerism, 6–7, 35–36
corporate-driven agenda and aid for
development, 2–3
cultural heterogeneity, 6

De Grauwe, Anton (1991), 26, 27, 46
democratic communism, 31–41;
alternative model to identity-based
liberal matrix, 37; cosmopolitanism
and, 37; democratic dialogue
considerations in, 38–39, 42n2;
democratic liberalism and, 39;
democratic social relations in, 38,
43n3; "dictatorship of the
proletariat", 33; direct democracy
and, 33–34; "embourgeoisement"
and, 31–32, 40–41; globalization
and, 35–37;
interpellation/embourgeois of social
actors, 32–33, 37–41; versus liberal
cosmopolitanism/identity politics,
34; liberation of the oppressed,
39–40; organic solidarity and, 34–35;
political reconfiguration in, 40–41;
social means of production in, 41;
socialization in post-industrial
capitalism, 33–37; the

structure/agency problematic in,
31–33; "ultimate ethical end" in, 40,
41
development aid and the corporate-
driven agenda, 2–3
dialogical pedagogy, 38
"dictatorship of the proletariat", 39
Domhoff, William (2002), vii, 2, 46
Dreeben, Robert and Rebecca Barr
(1983), 17, 46
Durkheim, Emile (1984 [1893]), 32, 47

economic bifurcation, 7
economic hybrids: in globalization, 36;
legitimization of, 12; as pawns for
capital, 8–9
education: American policy goals and, 23;
Black English Vernacular and, 17, 18,
19, 20, 21; blacks in capitalist
education, 16–17; bourgeois capitalists
and, 1; Caribbean enterprise culture
and, 24; cultural sites in opposition to
capitalist education, 8; failure of black
children in, 15–16; as an ideological
state apparatus, 4, 6, 8, 18, 28;
marginalization of Blacks in, 17; as a
neutral process, 7; post-industrial
capitalist purpose of, 8–9; role of in
post-industrial age, 7–8; and selves, 1;
"Standard English" and American
Blacks, 16, 18, 20, 21; student
subjectivity and, 12. *See also* (post)
industrial pedagogy in U.S.; (post)
modern pedagogy
"embourgeoisement", 6, 15, 21, 31–32
"embourgeoisement" of the masses,
40–41
embourgeois/interpellation of social
actors, 32–33, 37–41
Erevelles, Nirmala (2000), 6, 7, 8, 35,
47

financial expansion, 7
Florida Comprehensive Assessment Test
(FCAT), 20

Ford, Donna Y. and J. John Harris
(1996), 19, 47
Fordham, Signithia and John Ogbu
(1986), 16, 19, 47
Frazier, Franklin E. (1957), 15, 47
Freire, Paulo (2000 [1970]), 1, 2, 28, 37,
47, 48
Freire, Paulo, Manichean polarity of, 39
Freire, Paulo on oppressor and
oppressed, 37–38
Freirean dialogical practices, 8, 9
Freireian pedagogical practices in
education, 36

Giddens, Anthony (1984), 32, 48
Giddens, Anthony (1990), 6, 35
Giroux, Henry, 31, 37, 38
Giroux, Henry (1992), 7, 24, 35, 48
Glazer, Nathan and Daniel P. Moynihan,
(1963), 15, 48
"global social democracy", 34
globalization: as a condition of U.S.
capitalist organization, 6, 35;
consumerism and, 6–7, 35–36;
critical social theory and, 41n1;
defined, 3, 42n2; Democratic
communism and, 35–37; educational
pedagogical practices and, 6–9,
12n1; "ideological state apparatuses"
and, ix, 6; neoliberalism and, 3;
Protestant ethic and, 13n2; scientific
management movement and, 9;
scientific/technological revolutions
and, 13n2; social structure of
inequality in, 2–6. *See also* Granada;
pedagogy in globalization
Gramsci, Antonio quoted on the
ordinary mass of people, 39–40
Granada: Basic Education Reform Project
of, 29n3; the bureaucracy of, 28;
educational pedagogy in, 26–27, 29;
exploitation of its labor force, 28;
foreign investment in, 27; ideological
state apparatuses and, 28; industries in
percentage of GDP in, *29;* Maurice

Bishop and administration of, 25–26;
New Jewel Movement in, 25; People's
Revolutionary Government (PRG),
major aims of, 26, 27; U.S. invasion
of, 26; work-study program in, 26,
43n4. *See also* Caribbean nations,
supply side economics and

Habermas, Jürgen, 31, 34, 35, 38, 39,
40, 41
Habermas, Jürgen (1984), viii, 3, 48
Habermas, Jürgen (1984 [1981]), 4, 32,
48
Habermas, Jürgen (1987 [1981]), 4, 48
Habermas, Jürgen (1996, 1998), 34
Harding, Neil (1997), 40, 48
Harvey, David (1989), 6, 35, 48
Held, David, 31, 34, 35, 37, 38, 39, 40,
41
Held, David (1995, 2005), 34
Held, David (2004; 2005), 34
Hickling-Hudson, Anne (1988), 26, 38,
48
human identity of the oppressed, 39–40

identity politics, 34
ideological apparatuses: American
Blacks and, 18; democratic, 38;
democratic social relations and, 38,
42n2; education, 4, 5; globalization
and, ix, 6; in Granada, 28; human
identity and, 39; intellectual elites
and, 39; "technical rationality" of the
oppressor and, 39, 43n4
IMF 2001 Report, Granada Industries in
Percentage of GDP, *29*
industrial production expansion, 7, 9
International Monetary Fund (IMF), 2
interpellation/embourgeois of social
actors, 32–33, 37–41

Jameson, Fredric (1991), 6, 35, 49

Kellner, Douglas (2001), 6, 35, 49
Klak, et al. (1998), 27

Klak, Thomas (1998), viii, 3, 49
knowledge and the structure of history,
    38

labor: cheap labor, 3; economic
    bifurcation and, 7; exploitation of,
    28, 36, 37; reorganization of, 11–12;
    revamped role of, 10–12; scientific
    management movement and, 9–10;
    "soft skills" and, 11, 24
Labov, William (1972), 17, 18, 20, 49
*Language in the Inner-City: Studies in
    the Black English Vernacular*,
    William Labov, 17, 19
Lenin, Vladimir, 39
liberal cosmopolitanism, 34, 37
Lupel, (2005), 34

management-initiated employee
    involvement programs (EIPs), 12
McLaren, Peter, 38
McLaren, Peter (1988), 7, 35, 50
McMichael, Phillip (1996), VIII, 3, 50
Mocombe, Paul (2001), 2, 10, 50
Murray, (1984), 16, 19

neoliberal logic, 24
neoliberalism, 3

Ogbu, John (1974, 1990, 1991), 19, 50
Ogbu, John on racial marginalization,
    16
ontological security, 6
organic solidarity, 32, 34–35

pedagogy (dialogical), 38
pedagogy and globalization: American
    policy goals and, 23; Caribbean
    enterprise culture and, 24; "soft
    skills" and, 24; supply side
    economics and, 24
pedagogy of the oppressed, 37–38
Pedagogy of the Oppressed (2000
    [1977]), Paulo Freire, 37

Portes, Alejandro (1997), viii, 3, 50
(post) industrial pedagogy in U.S.:
    effect on labor, 10; management-
    initiated employee involvement
    programs (EIPs) and, 12;
    reorganization of labor and, 10,
    11–12; restructuring of American
    capitalist society and, 10–11; role of
    subcultures in, 9; scientific
    management movement and, 9–10;
    socialization of *Being* in capitalism,
    11–12, 13n3
(post) modern pedagogy: class hierarchy
    of capitalism and, 8; consumerism
    and, 7, 8; cultural heterogeneity and,
    6; economic bifurcation and, 7;
    economic hybrids and, 7, 8–9;
    Freirean dialogical practices in, 8, 9;
    social failure of, 7–8; U.S. hegemony
    and, 6, 8
"prescription", defined, 37
profit, 7, 11
Protestant ethic: agency, 4, 8, 15;
    American Blacks and, 15; discourse,
    ix, 2, 5; economic hybrids and, 36;
    globalization and, 13n2; social
    ontology of, 31–32

reified consciousness, 2, 42n2

Saussure de, Ferdinand (1986 [1960]),
    5, 50
Schooling in Capitalist America,
    Samuel Bowles and Herbert Gintis, 8
Schwalbe, Michael L. (1993), 1, 50
scientific management movement,
    9–10
semiotic field of society, 5
Sennett, Richard (1998), 10, 50
Sklair, Leslie (2001), 6, 35, 50
Smith, Vicki (1998), 10, 11, 51
social ontology, 31–32, 39, 42n3
socialization in post-industrial
    capitalism, 1, 33–37, 33–37

society, semiotic field of, *5*
sociolinguistics and American Blacks education, 17–21
sociological fallacy, 17
"soft skills", 11, 24
solidarity: mechanical, 32; organic, 32, 34–35
Sowell, Thomas (1975, 1981), 16, 19, 51
spirit of capitalism, 2, 4, 5, 31
Springs, Joel (1994), 10, 51
Standard English and American Blacks, 16, 18, 20, 21, 22n2
structure/agency problematic, 31–33
supply side economics, 24

Taylor, Frederick Winslow, 9
"technical rationality" of the oppressor, 39, 43n4
test taking, 13n3, 15, 16, 17, 19
Trichur, (2005), 7
Tye, Kenneth A. (1999), 6, 12n1, 51
Tyson et al. (2005), 16, 17

United States: hegemony of, 3; invasion of Granada, 26; (post) modern pedagogy and, 6
U.S. Department of Education (2003), 18, 22nn3-4, 51

Van Hook, Jennifer (2002), 17, 51

Wallerstein, (1974), viii, 6
Wallerstein, Immanuel (1974), 51
Wallerstein, Immanuel, world-systems theory of, 3, 31, 35
Watson, (1997), 24
Weber, Max (1946), 33
Weber, Max (1958), 5, 52
Weber, Max on leveling of the governed, 33
Who Rules America, William Domhoff, 2, 46
Wilson, William J. (1978), 15, 18, 52
work, reorganization of, 10–12
World Bank, 2
World Trade Organization (WTO), 2